Reasons I Should Have Become a Nun

Reasons I Should Have Become a Nun

A Dating Confessional

Mary Katharine O'Shae

Copyright © 2020 Mary Katharine O'Shae
All rights reserved. No part of this book may be reproduced, stored in or introduced into a retrieval system or transmitted in any form or by any means (electronic, photocopying, recording, mechanical or otherwise), without prior permission in writing from the author except by a reviewer who may quote brief passages in a review.

ISBN-13: 978-1-7341283-0-7

DEDICATION

To all the boys and men I have dated before,
and those yet to encounter all that I am.

ACKNOWLEDGMENTS

I would like to thank Maria Bea Divine for all her time and effort in bringing this book to fruition. Without her support and encouragement, it would have never happened. She spent hours helping edit and refine the stories. Laughing and crying with me. Helping me heal and getting me ready to get out there again. She is inspirational, relentless, and full of unconditional love. Her positivity and bright outlook on life is contagious and necessary to balance my doomsday outlook on life.

Thank you to all my friends who were there on the day to day with the dates and relationships. Helping me find those big girl panties to pull up to get back out there.

PROLOGUE

Growing up, I truly believed that my relationships would conform to the following steps:

1. Date though college
2. Get married to a wonderful man – my best friend
3. Have beautiful children with my best friend
4. Retire with my best friend - soulmate

I never dreamed that after 35 years I would still be stuck on step 1. And it's not because I didn't try!

Before I go on, I define a date as two people meeting in person at a given place, at a given time that is mutually agreed upon. That being said, I have been on a grand total of 582 first dates. 201 made the second date. 105 survived a third date, 48 graduated into 4+ dates, and 10 progressed into the relationship stage of more than three months.

Dating is a lot like job hunting. The first date is the interview. Both parties are hoping that the other is "the one" because no one likes to go on interviews or conduct them. Can you imagine going on 582 job interviews??

Even if you get the job, there are no guarantees that you will keep it. You can quit (break up) or get fired (divorce) or decide to stay because the benefits are good.

So, I have decided to share with you some of my more colorful experiences. The boring ones are left out because if the date is boring, the story will follow suit. Besides, who wants to read about the standard "I'm not ready to commit," or "I'm not over my ex," etc. At times, they were total nut jobs and, at times, I was the total nut job. I will let you know which is which, but you can make your own judgment.

You will also see patterns in my dysfunctional choices and what I was willing to put up with for the "comfort" of being in a relationship. Most of the names have been changed. Thanks to social media, we can now track people and find out what happened to them. And don't try to drunk dial any of the phone numbers. I hope you catch the humor in the ones I chose.

Now, I invite you all to delve into my world of career dating. Read it for a laugh or a cry or share with your friends on girls' night along with several bottles of wine. I'm sure many of you have known a "Handy Hank" or an "Earthy Earl." Sometimes I think it would have been easier to choose Jesus as my husband. But then these stories wouldn't exist, and you would have nothing to read!

PREFACE TO THE HIGH SCHOOL YEARS

I went to a K through 8 Catholic school with the same 20 kids in my class. Unlike some of my classmates, I never had a boyfriend during those years. Of course, we did play Spin the Bottle in the basement and Three Minutes in Heaven in random closets, but no real kiss. That's just part of every good Catholic school upbringing. And at that point in time, who didn't have a crush on Shaun Cassidy, Rob Lowe, C. Thomas Howell, and Ralph Macchio?

My cousin (who was the same age as me) claimed to have already made out with boys before high school, and she felt that I needed to do the same. So right after I graduated from grade school, on our family's annual 4th of July camping trip, she pushed me off on this guy we met at the campgrounds. He took me for a walk and planted my first kiss. It was gross. He was a smoker and had a mushy tongue. I just did it to get that first kiss over with. And peer pressure. Thank goodness Hank came along.

Handy Hank   **Him**

When I was 10, Hank and his brother Joseph used to pick on me because I was chubby. My mom would drag me across the street to tell their parents that they were picking on me. I could hear their parents yelling at them as we walked back home... which of course made me feel like an even chubbier jerk! Thanks, Mom!!!

Three years later, I had grown four inches taller, was 25 pounds lighter, and became date-worthy in Hank's eyes. Just before my 14th birthday, I went on my very first date with Hank. I remember this day so vividly because it was my first real introduction to what boys want. We double-dated with the previously mentioned cousin and her date, a former classmate of mine who lived around the corner. I wore a white t-shirt and a pair of pink and white striped seersucker shorts with my pink Chucks (aka Converse low tops).

We went to see "Purple Rain." As we were watching the movie, his hand started on my knee, then crept up to my thigh, and then underneath my shorts. Oh my! I swatted his hand away. Why oh why did he think it was okay to try to feel me up in the movies? Of course, I know NOW! He was a horny 15-year-old boy! He completely bypassed the boobs and went straight for the big V! I didn't know at the time that my pink shorts had a sign on them that said, "Touch me here!" YIKES!!! Sex education didn't exist in Catholic grammar school. I didn't even know what those parts were really for yet. My sex education was my father reading me the riot act after he saw me kissing Hank in our bathing suits in the backyard. He was only touching my arm and shoulder. I'm so glad he didn't see us in the movies!

We dated until the end of my first month in high school. He broke it off and started dating a friend of mine. Since this was my first shot at dating, I got over it pretty fast. A few years later, his brother Joseph developed a crush on me and we had a one-night make-out session on my porch during a thunderstorm. It was fun for what it was.

I ran into Hank years later. He never married but has a girlfriend and kids. He's doing his dream job as a fishing instructor. In the off-season, he works with my aunt's sister-in-law at a gas station convenience store. He seems very happy and often mentions to her that he used to date me. Very sweet, but that crush is long dead and gone.

HIGH SCHOOL HIGHLIGHTS

My sex education expanded once I started high school. We weren't allowed to have boys in our bedrooms, but we could sit in the family room in the basement with a TV, stereo, and Atari. Many of the houses in this blue-collar neighborhood had the same setup with the finished basement. We managed to do enough making out and holding hands down there, even though my parents' bedroom and the laundry room were also in the basement. Fortunately, the door leading to the basement would creak whenever it was opened, which kept us from getting caught! In addition to the aforementioned crushes, there was The Edge from U2, James Spader (bad boy), Val Kilmer, and Ducky (John Cryer) – he had great hair and eyes. And John Stamos on "General Hospital".

Roller Rink Rick   **Neither**

I was now in the middle of my freshman year and I had finally turned 14. It was the 1980s, and one of our favorite pastimes was roller-skating. Plus, it was a great place to meet boys. This particular night was a heavily chaperoned overnight skate for teens. I went with my sister and her friends. She was a sophomore, so I guess my parents thought she would look after me. Not so much.

Rick was a freshman in college – ooohh, an older boy! He was skinny with brown hair and carried a comb in his back pocket. So hot!!! He came up to me. We started talking. He asked me to skate and then held my hand. He skated backwards. I still can't. We sat along the side of the rink on the little step and it was there he kissed me. We skated, we kissed. We skated; we kissed some more. Sadly, the night ended. He had to go back to COLLEGE!

Luckily, Rick's brother sat in front of me in most of my classes – thanks, alphabetical seating! He would pass notes back and forth for us. I'm sure he read them; I would have!

Rick and I had endless conversations over the phone. We finally had a first date and went to the movies. Then it just faded. I was too young for a long-distance relationship. A few years later I was thinking, "Hmmm, college freshman dating a high school freshman is a little odd." But as a 14-year-old girl, I thought I was cool, and so did my friends.

Charming Charlie   **Me**
The One Who Got Away #1
Charlie was Hank's best friend. I was a sophomore; he was a junior. He was tall, cute, brown hair and eyes, a great smile, and was sweeter than anything.

For our first "official" date, his dad gave us hockey tickets and passes to the private dining club at the ice rink. I got all dressed up, sporting a total '80s look with a plaid dress, poufier-than-poufy hair, and two-toned heeled boots. I can laugh now about how silly I must have looked.

Growing up in a working-class family, our idea of fine dining was a Friday night fish fry or The Ground Round with free popcorn and peanuts. Needless to say, at this dining club, I was a bit clueless. The salad leaves were huge. I was used to shredded lettuce, a cherry tomato, and a big glob of Russian dressing. I kept fumbling and fumbling until Charlie said, "Why don't you just cut it?" All I thought was, "You can cut salad?" It feels silly to even write it now, but at the time I was truly embarrassed.

Over the next few months, Charlie and I spent most of the time in the basement making out and watching TV. Why did I break up with him? Oh yes, Bold Billy (see below). Gosh dang it! That only lasted a month, then I wanted Charlie back. Surprise! He didn't want me! He went for another girl in our church group. I was devastated.

After Charlie graduated, he went into the military. We did make out one final time, when he was on leave. That was the last time I saw him. I would take him back today, but he is happily married, has a great job and a beautiful family. I am happy for him.

Bold Billy — Him

So, the guy I dumped Charlie for was Bold Billy. He was on the wrestling team, but not as smart as Charlie. I don't think there was ever a first date. We would walk around school and hold hands. On the phone, we would simultaneously hit 'play' on the tape deck to listen and sing to "Stairway to Heaven" together. We kissed a lot, and he tried touching – in particular, my boobs any chance he got.

One time we were in the basement when my family was away for the day, and he graduated from boobs to that other lovely lady part. But at this point I was only experimenting with above-the-clothes touching and wasn't ready to go beyond that point. He broke up with me for no good reason, except maybe I wouldn't allow him under the clothes.

I recently found him on social media. Definitely dodged a bullet on that one!

Brother Benjamin
The One Who Got Away #1-1/2

Neither

After my freshman year, my best friend Anna moved to another state. I went to visit her over Easter Break in my sophomore year. On my first night there, her brother Benjamin came home from work and joined us in Anna's room, where we were catching up. She went to sleep in the top bunk bed. Ben and I stayed up late and continued talking. His mother must have heard us laughing. She came in and found us lying on the lower bunk, with me under the covers and him on top. For real!! She yelled at him to get back to bed. I was mortified. I had broken the "No boys in the bedroom" rule. And on DAY ONE! I had the rest of the week with the family to look forward to. UGH!!

Benjamin and I went to the movies on a double date with Anna and her boyfriend Doug. During most of the movie they were in a full-on make-out straddling session. Ben and I just kind of sunk low in our seats, pretending we were not with them.

The last night before I flew home, Doug's parents were out of town. He decided to throw a party at his house. We were all just hanging around, drinking, and watching Pink Floyd's "The Wall." Benjamin and I started making out. I don't remember how much vodka I drank or how I got so many hickeys. Thanks, Benjamin! But I do remember him being with me in the bathroom as I was puking, and his mom taking care of me for the rest of the night. The next morning, I lied and told her, "I get nervous saying goodbye and flying." I doubt she bought that excuse – and I'm sure she knew it was her son that mutilated my neck.

When I returned home, I tried to hide all the love bites. Unfortunately, it wasn't turtleneck weather. Yes, my father saw them and yes, I got in trouble and yes, he still let me go back a few more times during my high school years. What were our parents thinking???

Benjamin always had girlfriends when I went back, so nothing more happened. He joined the military after high school. I saw him one more time at Anna's wedding. I was in her bridal party. Last I knew, he was married with two kids and still in the service. Benjamin was a terrific guy but not enough of a possibility for me to consider him one of the ones who got away, well maybe a half ...

Not-So-Stand-Up Catholic Boy   **Him**

We met at a CYO (Catholic Youth Organization) convention. He was geeky cute – tall, thin, a U2 kind of haircut. First date was great... he picked me up and we took a walk in the park. Then non-stop talking on the phone for two weeks (which at 16 was an ETERNITY!). Second date, he stood me up. Amen.

Sincere Sam   **Me**
The One Who Got Away #2
Sam wanted to date me, but I rejected him because he was "not my type" physically. He was a super-nice, sweet guy – just a little chubby. And this is coming from someone who used to be a chubby girl. How crazy is that?! Not so nice on my part. He was on the football team, Vice President of the Student Union, and liked by everyone. He was a senior. I was a sophomore. Of course, as soon as he started dating this really cute girl, I wanted him. But it was too late. When he came home from college freshman year, we went out a few times. Nothing came of it. I cyberstalked him recently and found out we had the same major. He is married now, and I hope he is happy.

Senior Prom – You Have to Go, Right?   **Neither**
I didn't go to Junior Prom because I wasn't asked and the guy I asked never got back to me. Checked him out on social media. Let's just say that karma exists. I still look freakin' awesome and him not so much.

I went to the Senior Prom with a guy in study hall because neither one of us had a date. I looked typically ridiculous – I mean, it was the '80s! My aunt did my hair – a huge bouffant football helmet. Not at all cute, adorable, sexy, or attractive.

My family didn't have much money, so I wore a red and white strapless gown we purchased from a discount store. I loved red so it was okay, although it did look more like a bridesmaid's dress. My sister wound up wearing it for a prom five years later.

The best part of the prom was the limo. It was my first-time riding in one, and I got to share it with my best friends. There was no alcohol, so the ride was rather boring. The prom wasn't much better. I didn't even dance with my date, and there was no goodnight kiss either. Just recently I discovered we are actually Facebook friends.

At least the prom picnic was less boring. One of my guy friends got so drunk he puked down the inside of my car door. We dropped him off about three blocks from his house. Later that night, his mom called worried about him. We walked around looking for him and found him passed out on the middle school lawn. He got grounded.

COLLEGE YEARS

High school was meh. It was fun and I made the most of it, but I was ready to move on to the next adventure. I lived at home while going to college. Even though my parents were strict in some ways, we were good kids so we were given a lot of freedom. I didn't really want to go to college. I don't even know why I didn't want to go. I just didn't see the relevance. My dad didn't go, nor did many of my relatives. But my parents said skipping college was not an option.

By the time I started classes and became involved in the college radio station, I realized I was excited to be there. I switched majors several times – communications, political science, then finally settling on mathematics. It was a marketable degree I could take anywhere in the world.

I had caught the travel bug that summer when I went on a group trip to Italy and France with the high school's foreign language teacher. A math degree, I figured, would let me live anywhere.

In college, when I took acting classes and performed in a few plays, I knew that's what I wanted to do. I had acted in grammar school plays every year, but not in high school. They only did musicals and people would pay for me not to sing. But the passion was there for regular theater. I loved it. So, I could use my math degree to bankroll my acting career. BINGO.

Now back to the dating stories through college. Val Kilmer was still a hottie and Tom Cruise hadn't become creepy yet. And then on the music scene – Prince (of course!) and John Linnell from They Might Be Giants. Something about musicians.

A Tale of Two Toms   Him/Me

Oh, how I liked Nasty Tom. Oh, how Nice Tom liked me. This made for interesting calls when one of my sisters would answer the phone and say it was Tom. I always had to wait to hear his first words to know which Tom I was talking to. This was obviously before Caller ID.

Nice Tom had funky teeth and was a little gooberish but a much, much nicer guy overall. We never officially dated as far as I was concerned, but he might have thought differently about the numerous times we hung out together. But we never even kissed.

Nasty Tom always sniffled but had great hair and beautiful eyes. I am a sucker for big hair, big eyes, and big teeth. My mom always joked that I chose boyfriends like I was buying a horse.

So, I chose to lose my virginity to Nasty Tom while I was housesitting for a friend. On top of that, I had a broken leg. It was awkward. No, VERY awkward. Not at all romantic, and no surprise it wasn't fulfilling either. I wish it had been someone else, because soon afterwards Nasty Tom broke up with me. He said I was "too young" for him – only then he started dating someone even younger. Bastard. He wanted to "friend" me on social media recently, and I declined. I'm not being petty, but I just don't care. However, I did friend Nice Tom and karma seems to have rewarded him with a pretty wife and what seems like a very fulfilling life.

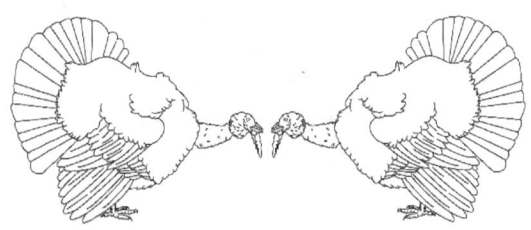

Provocative Paul   Neither

I met Provocative Paul on campus. He was skinny and had a nice smile, curly brown hair, and an acceptable mullet for the era. He was charming and knew how to say just the right things. We had lunch a few times and made out in the Student Union before we had our one and only official date. We saw "The Little Mermaid" then snuck into a nearby park that was a big teenage hangout on weekends. We walked around and had a steamy make-out session in the woods.

Unfortunately, Paul had a bit of a reputation for being a "ladies' man." So, I decided to take a pass on him. He is now happily married with a family, and still has that great smile. A lot less hair, but still that great smile!

Prudent Paul   Neither
The One Who Got Away #3

The opposite of Provocative Paul was Prudent Paul. He was straight and narrow. He was musically inclined which is (almost) always hot. I was friends with him and his girlfriend but was happy when they broke up.

He was in a total '80s/'90s alternative garage band. I recently found an autograph from them when I was cleaning out stuff. They played at the Elks and Moose Lodges and were fantastic!

Prudent Paul had spiked blonde hair and glasses – an average Joe, but he just rocked my socks off. After his breakup, we started hanging out more. After a few dates and a lot of making out, I decided I wanted to do a little more than kissing. However, he seemed very uncomfortable with my advances and ended it.

I wish things had developed with him because he was a sweet and honest guy. He is happily married with a beautiful family. Yay!

Earthy Earl   **Neither**

I went to New Zealand for a semester of college. I was able to travel about half of the time I was there, and I met Earl on one of these trips. He was from Fishkill, New York, but studying in Colorado Springs to be a forest ranger. Remember what my mom said about my dating is like buying a horse? All checked out - he was earthy with brown hair, big eyes, and a great smile. I thought he was cute and sweet.

After I returned to the States, we both happened to be in New York City at the same time. We had a great day walking around the city. He was an excellent tour guide. He took me to a little bodega and introduced me to Shawarma. Later, we went to see a Broadway show with his family. Then we all had dinner at Tad's Steakhouse, which still exists today. Whenever I walk past it, I think of him. He's a fond memory. We kept in touch for a while, but he lived so far away. It would have been nice to see if something could have developed. These days he is living in Montana, fulfilling his goal of being Mr. Forest Ranger.

Aussie Alex   **Neither ????**

During my stay in New Zealand, I took a fabulous 30-and-under type tour of the Australian Outback. I met some awesome people and the tour was amazing. I had mentioned to the tour guide that I wanted to visit Tasmania at the end of my semester. He said his brother Alex lived there and would be more than willing to show me around. So, I wrote to Alex (pre-email era), and for no reason at all (well maybe one – "wink wink"), he agreed.

I was thrilled when he picked me up in his dad's Jaguar, my favorite car because it looked like an old-school Dairy Queen banana split container. And then there was Alex himself – an Aussie Rules football player, which explained the fabulous body. He had curly dirty blonde hair, full lips, and an amazing smile. Yeah, I think I was mushy from the get-go.

Alex still lived with his parents, and we stayed there my first night in Tasmania. That evening we went to the casino with his friends and got completely shitfaced. We took a taxi back to his house, thank God. The passion started in the back seat on the ride home. We continued in the living room, but we were either too drunk or not drunk enough to seal the deal. When it was time to go to bed, I accidently stumbled into his parent's bedroom and woke them up. Just a little embarrassing. Thank goodness we were leaving the next day.

We camped in rented trailers, and he showed me around Tasmania. He was a great tour guide and we had lots of fun. He introduced me to Tracy Chapman, whom I enjoy to this day, and hearing her songs brings back fond memories. And yes, the "wink-wink" happened!

Alex and I kept in touch for the next few years while I finished college. After I graduated, he came to the U.S. and we traveled for six months in a Chevy Cavalier with a turtle top. We mostly camped or slept in the car. On a few occasions, we stayed in a motel. One time we were kicked off a Native American Reservation, and another time we were asked to leave a parking lot. Luckily, they came when they did to give us the boot. Minutes before we would have been caught in a very awkward position.

We were having a blast. We went to so many national parks, up and down the coasts, across the Rockies and through Canada. It was an amazing opportunity to see the country. Spending so much time together, both physically and intimately, he became my first love.

About five months into our trip, we stopped in L.A. to pick up his friends from the Aussie Rules football league. Apparently, Alex wanted to show off his manhood in front of his friends by being rude and demeaning to me. He actually threw something at me one night. Even his friends made a comment to him about it. When we dropped them off in Park City, Utah, he went back to being his old self. I should have dropped his ass off as well. But alas, I was young, stupid, and in love. Also, I knew our time together was ending in a couple of weeks.

So, Alex went off to England for six months and then returned to Australia. The letters dwindled over the years. He has a rather unique name so I searched for him on the Internet and found him in Tasmania. I wrote him a letter and received an email back. Not from him but from someone claiming that Alex was now his "boy toy." I thought he was pulling my leg so I asked to send pictures. I meant a picture of the two of them together, not "TOGETHER." Oh boy, did his boyfriend go off on me:

"Aussie Alex is now MY boy toy and who are YOU to ask for such things! Obviously, you and Alex weren't close enough for him to even tell you he was out of the closet." I still have no idea if he was really gay or if someone was having a good one at my expense. I tried to Facebook friend him, but he never accepted the request.

Alex and I kept in touch for the next few years while I finished college. After I graduated, he came to the U.S. and we traveled for six months in a Chevy Cavalier with a turtle top. We mostly camped or slept in the car. On a few occasions, we stayed in a motel. One time we were kicked off a Native American Reservation, and another time we were asked to leave a parking lot. Luckily, they came when they did to give us the boot. Minutes before we would have been caught in a very awkward position.

We were having a blast. We went to so many national parks, up and down the coasts, across the Rockies and through Canada. It was an amazing opportunity to see the country. Spending so much time together, both physically and intimately, he became my first love.

About five months into our trip, we stopped in L.A. to pick up his friends from the Aussie Rules football league. Apparently, Alex wanted to show off his manhood in front of his friends by being rude and demeaning to me. He actually threw something at me one night. Even his friends made a comment to him about it. When we dropped them off in Park City, Utah, he went back to being his old self. I should have dropped his ass off as well. But alas, I was young, stupid, and in love. Also, I knew our time together was ending in a couple of weeks.

So, Alex went off to England for six months and then returned to Australia. The letters dwindled over the years. He has a rather unique name so I searched for him on the Internet and found him in Tasmania. I wrote him a letter and received an email back. Not from him but from someone claiming that Alex was now his "boy toy." I thought he was pulling my leg so I asked to send pictures. I meant a picture of the two of them together, not "TOGETHER." Oh boy, did his boyfriend go off on me:

"Aussie Alex is now MY boy toy and who are YOU to ask for such things! Obviously, you and Alex weren't close enough for him to even tell you he was out of the closet." I still have no idea if he was really gay or if someone was having a good one at my expense. I tried to Facebook friend him, but he never accepted the request.

20s AND OUT OF COLLEGE

It was time to leave my hometown and set off on some new adventures! I had already traveled to New Zealand/ Australia, across the USA and to Europe, so I knew there was a whole world out there for me to explore.

I dreamed about living in Seattle with its beautiful Craftsman houses, parks, ocean, Puget Sound... so, I moved there. I fell in love with the city along with the wonders of the wine country and the mountains. It was the '90s and a fantastic time to live there.

I found a great group of friends. It was one amazing day after another. I was excited to be in a new city with new experiences just waiting for me to discover them. I had no idea what I would encounter in the dating world.

Who was attractive in my twenties? Still had that thing for Val Kilmer, and then Matt Damon came around and there was just something about him. And "ER" with Noah Wyle.

Complicated Clyde   **Me**
The One Who Got Away #4

I dated Clyde for about six months. My first boyfriend in the new town I moved to, Seattle. Well, sort-of boyfriend – we were exclusive but never called each other boyfriend/girlfriend. Why? Mostly because of me.

He was eager and suffered from SMS (Short Man Syndrome aka Napoleon Complex). He wanted to be a doctor and worked really hard at it. He was always nice and supportive of me. He had a lot of issues he was dealing with – or should I say not dealing with – from his upbringing and his parents. Looking back, who really dealt with things in their early twenties... especially a guy?

I really liked being around him but wasn't keen on him living with his ex-girlfriend's father and thought I could do better. Plus, he didn't have a lot of friends, so that should tell me something, right?

At the six-month mark, I broke up with him as I really didn't want it to go anywhere. Then, of course, I got jealous when he started dating this other girl at work. She of course regarded me as a threat and wouldn't let us be friends. Why do we always want someone back once someone new enters their lives?

Nowadays, I wonder how he is doing. If I could only remember his last name, I would stalk – ahem, research – him too! I wish I had let this one develop more without so much judgment.

Straight Male Gay Bar Dancer Don   Neither
Don was a dancer at a gay bar. Totally HOT. Did I say HOT? Slender, fit, and to find out later "wink, wink" very straight!!

I met him at a bar, we started chatting and totally hit it off. I was a little stunned that someone like him asked me for my phone number – and even more stunned when he actually called! He took me to a vegetarian Chinese restaurant and brought me flowers.

Sadly, after a few dates he told me he was moving back to Utah or Colorado or one of those mountain states. I was bummed, but it was fun while it lasted. Most importantly, he taught me it was good to giggle and communicate during sex.

Valentine's Date   **Me**

I don't remember his name and I don't remember how we met. But I do remember he was sweet and I do remember that I was an ASS for not going out with him again.

Our first and last date was Valentine's Day. He showed up at my door with a cheap box of drug store chocolates wrapped in red cellophane and flowers. Really? He made up for it by taking me to my favorite restaurant in the city and ordering a bottle of champagne. I have only good memories of this date, but at the time I wasn't feeling it. Why did I let him go? Oh, I couldn't get past the red cellophane drug store chocolates. Alas, to be in your twenties and think the world is your oyster and so many more are to come. Once again, judgment got in the way... and did I mention I was the ASS of all ASSES?

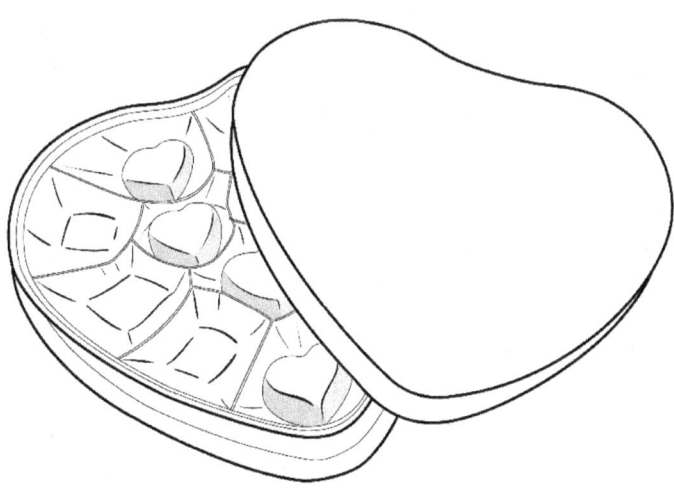

New Year's Nate — Him

It was New Year's Eve and I was out with a few friends at a local bar. Good music, good conversation, good drinks!! I spent most of the evening talking to Nate. He looked like the boy next door: average height, average weight, average looks. As the clock struck midnight, he grabbed me and kissed me. It was one of those magical movie moments. He asked for my number... and he called!

On our first date, he took me to dinner at a great restaurant overlooking Puget Sound. He told me he was the great-grandson of the guy who started a particular beer brand that has recently made a comeback with hipsters. However, he was not a TFB (Trust Fund Baby) because his grandmother was the youngest and pretty much got nothing. He had been on a work-exchange program in Belgium, where he had a steady girlfriend, but then broke it off when he returned. I, in turn, divulged way too much information about my life. It freaked him out, so there was no second date. I needed to learn not to say too much, but I have such logorrhea.

Italian Stallion Dario — Him

I met Dario at a wine tasting event with my friend Maggie. He had dark hair, olive skin, big brown eyes, and a nice body. It's amazing I didn't remember what his teeth looked like, him being a stallion and all. We had a few good dates, but all he wanted to do was fool around and I told him I wanted more. We double-dated with Maggie and her boyfriend. They thought he was an arrogant ass. He was. It ended when he didn't call me when he got back from an L.A. trip. I was pissed. I thought he would eventually come around. My mistake – this was a no-expectation relationship. Ugh.

Funny Filipino Freddy   Him

My friend Jackie did not want me to spend Thanksgiving alone so she invited me to her parents' house. There I met Funny Filipino Freddy. He lived in L.A. and was a producer on a comedy talk show. She insisted this wasn't a setup. Regardless, we really hit it off. We talked on the phone, emailed each other, and we had our first date when he returned to Seattle to visit his mom. We had a great time.

Eventually, he invited me to L.A. Everything was going well until we went to bed and started fooling around. I must have insulted his manhood when I started giggling. But I was just enjoying myself. He stopped and said, "You're not supposed to laugh." I said, "It tickled!" At that point he rolled over and went to sleep.

Breakfast was awkward. Whatever! He couldn't take me to the airport fast enough.

I saw him again a few years later back at Jackie's parents' house. We were civil but no real conversation. Freddy needed to take some lessons from Dancer Don. Sex should be fun – not work, and not so serious!

Irish Innocence of Kind Kieran   Neither
Love of My Life #1

While I was teaching, I would travel solo across Europe during my summer vacations. I usually stayed in youth hostels. I met Kieran as I was boarding a ferry from France to Dublin. He was tall and lanky, with brown hair. He seemed charming and very sincere. We started chatting, and I could see he was getting seasick. I clearly remember thinking "Do I stay with this guy or do I leave? I mean, he is sick, and that just wouldn't be nice." So, I stayed.

I told him my plan was to just visit the Ring of Kerry, but he insisted that I stay with him in Dublin for a few days. Of course, he still lived with his family. Luckily, his brother gave up his bedroom.

Kieran took me all around Dublin. He was really sweet. After the weekend, I left for the Ring of Kerry and we kept in touch.

The following summer, Kieran and I met in Copenhagen. The first night we slept in separate single beds in a small pensione. We spent the next day walking and biking around Copenhagen. Then the romance began in Tivoli Gardens when he grabbed my hand. For a moment, I wasn't sure if I was okay with this, but quickly decided I was. That night we pushed the beds together and simply cuddled and kissed. He didn't try anything more. It was a great vacation. I'm smiling as I write about it.

The next year, he came to visit me in Seattle and I fell in love. We went to wineries, played around Seattle, and just had a great time. This time we had "wink-wink" and it was amazing. We made a pact that if we were still single in our mid-thirties, we would get together. I still have my favorite picture of us at Willamette Valley Vineyards. I was behind him holding him around the neck. We are both smiling and very much in love.

We kept in touch over the years. I fantasized about moving to Ireland and we would live happily ever after. He did come back to visit me when Love of My Life #2 broke my heart. We cuddled and kissed again, but no more than that. He was there to be a good friend.

He returned home and started dating a woman named Amanda. I wasn't sure how serious it was, so I asked if he would be interested in meeting up somewhere again. He was mortified that I would suggest that. So that's when I knew it was serious and I had lost this love. They are now married and so in love. I am super happy for him. We don't keep in touch much anymore which is sad. That is one good thing about social media; I get to check up with him that way. Sad how friendships change over time.

Diggity Doggity Dan   **Me**
All I can remember about this date is being back at his place making out. It was horrible. I finally said, "Would you stop licking me like a dog??" He stopped for a bit then started up again. I got up and left. No second date for a man who can't even kiss well. That had to be the worst kiss I've ever had since my first kiss.

Prelude to Love of My Life #2
While I was out with Maggie, we met a bunch of guys having a bachelor party. Not only did we get a ride home in their limo, we got an invite to their friend's infamous annual holiday party which they said is always over the top.

I took some of my single friends and we had a blast. Maggie was talking with Harry, whom I also had my eye on. Here I must confess some little girl bitchiness. On the way home, I had the audacity to tell Maggie that "I backed down and let you have that guy." I can't help that I have a high opinion of myself – and still do. But what an asshole move on my part. They wound up dating for a few years. During that time, Harry introduced me to Lance.

Dropping Salsa Stoner Lance   Him*
Love of My Life #2
***But he was shitty on how he did it so extra boo!!!**
On our first date, a group of us went salsa dancing. Lance and I danced. He dropped me on the ground during the dips. Twice. The lesson learned is don't lead your own dip!

Maggie drove. We were in the front seat, Lance in the back. We sank down, debating whether or not I should take Lance home, assuming he couldn't hear us. Later, Lance told me he could hear everything. He didn't say a word because he was listening with every bone in his body to see if he would get lucky.

Well, he did. The next morning, however, I was leaving on vacation. He left me the sweetest message on my cell and offered to pick me up from the airport. And he DID! We started dating, but after six months I knew it wasn't right.

He never wanted to get married. I did. He said he didn't smoke a lot of pot. He did. In my world, once a day is a lot! He wanted more time with his friends. I wanted more time with him. There was give and take on both sides, but it was never enough for either of us. We were two different people trying to make it work. I told him once that I was a better catch than him. That didn't go over well! But we enjoyed each other's company, and the sex was great.

Around Valentine's Day, I met him in Whistler where he had been skiing with friends. Before I left, I cut my hair. It was to the mid back, long for me, and I got it cut to a chin-length bob. We women know how men are with women and their hair. He was not very happy. But he did get me a sleek, sexy Valentine's Day gift...a cellophane wrapped food sealer from the drug store in town after I arrived. What's up with Valentine's gifts involving cellophane?

Lance loved to rollerblade. Every week he participated in a "Saturday Night Skate." I tried the skate once but it scared the crap out of me. Up was hard, down was too fast. And I still can't skate backwards. On one of these skate nights, Harry collided into Lance. Boom! Lance busted out his knee. When he called, I hesitated about going to the hospital. Now, we had been together about a year and a half, so that tells you where our relationship was. I ended up going to the hospital and what did he do? He immediately handed me his bag of pot since none of his friends were there with him. I had wondered if he was getting high on the skate nights, and that confirmed it. I missed that red flag, big time.

I helped nurse him to wellness and carted his ass around, since he couldn't ride his motorcycle for a few months. He promised not to smoke pot while rollerblading after that.

But once he was back on the skates, his memory must have failed because he was back to smoking while skating. That did it! After two years, I had had enough. I ended it.

I was devastated and pathetically depressed. This was my first real relationship and break-up. I couldn't eat, sleep, and a day didn't go by without me crying hysterically for a good month. I don't even want to admit the psycho stuff I did. Well, okay, just a little. I checked his email only to find out he joined a dating site within a matter of weeks. I drove by his friend's house to see if his motorcycle was there. I followed him home and we ended up getting into a screaming fight in a park.

A few months passed and I started to move on. I had a few dates with a new guy. He came to see me in a play in which I played a leather-wearing, whip-carrying lesbian. I looked phenomenal due to the post break-up "exercise & depression diet." Of course, on that same night, Lance shows up. Surprise, he wanted to get back together!

I found out that Lance and a mutual friend of ours had fooled around after we broke up. During that time, she insisted to me that "it was for the best that we broke up and the next person I date will be my future husband." What a crock! From this point on, her nickname became Putana. I know it takes two to tango, but this "supportive" friend fed me this crap while trying to get him for herself. I should have let her have him!

He apologized, cried, and pleaded. He promised me he would quit smoking pot and prioritize time with me over his friends. I didn't ask him to change. He suggested it. He seemed so sincere that he was going to stick with it. He convinced himself this is what he wanted and that he could do it, so I believed him too. Everyone warned me that it wouldn't last. Again, I failed to listen to my friends.

From the beginning of our relationship, I had talked about moving to Los Angeles to pursue my dream of an acting career. I had spent time in Seattle studying and training by performing in plays, short films, and student films. I even had an agent. Lance never said much about it. When I decided to make the move, we agreed to give it one year and visit each other at least once a month. And that was exactly when his pot smoking started increasing again.

I was lucky to transfer with my job and found a great place to live. It all seemed rather perfect. Lance was supportive but didn't want to move to L.A. because he couldn't pursue his interests – rollerblading, mountain biking, skiing, and sailing. He actually said that!

He helped me move, but we were fighting a lot. My first few weeks in L.A. were spent getting acclimated to my new office, meeting new people, and getting my bearings. I was feeling a little antsy. A very close great-uncle of mine died. I had a dream in which Lance broke up with me. When I shared the dream and my concerns, he denied that breaking up was even a thought in his mind.

I went back to Seattle three weeks after my move. He was late picking me up at the airport but I let it go, and we had a pretty decent first night together. I went to the Seattle office the next morning to tie up some loose ends and after lunch, BOOM – I found out I was laid off!

Later that evening at Lance's apartment, we got into a big fight about my attitude. Yes, I was bitchy and upset because I had just moved to a new city and suddenly, I was jobless! No compassion on his end. The next day I asked him if he was okay, and he broke up with me. Stupid me tried to negotiate us getting back together. Thank goodness he stood his ground. He did me a favor.

Ten years later, I saw a social media post on a mutual friend's wall about how he has been with the love of his life for the last ten years. Hmmmm, we were still dating at that point.

THRILLING 30s

I left my twenties to begin a new decade of my life embarking on a new adventure in a new city. How would the Southern California men differ from the Pacific Northwest men? Ironically, my first two encounters were with Seattle men. Now in my thirties, Michael Bublé was up and coming... and oh, so cute and he can sing. Wentworth Miller had it going on in "Prison Break."

Tripod Tony   Me

Every time I went back to Seattle to visit my friends, we would always go to my favorite Italian restaurant. The place was beautiful, with stunning floor to ceiling windows. The gorgonzola and mushroom cream sauce served over mouth-melting gnocchi was always worth a visit. Seriously sensual, orgasmic food. The owner, Antonio, came to the United States illegally from Italy. He started as a dishwasher and worked his way up to busboy and then waiter. He ultimately bought the restaurant.

Antonio was short with gorgeous thick, black hair, and doe eyes. Another Italian Stallion! He was very cute and had a great Italian accent. Every time I came to the restaurant, he would ask me out. I always said no as I was there with my friends. On this particular night, my friends wanted to get home early to care for their baby. So, I agreed to meet Antonio at the restaurant at closing time.

Antonio brought out a magnificent bottle of Tuscan wine and some amazing desserts. Over the next two hours, he started getting touchy feely between sips of wine and bites of the whipped cream-covered desserts. I certainly didn't object. I wonder how many people walked by the place and saw us!

Suddenly, however, he whipped out Mr. Happy and says with his thick Italian accent, "Touch it and make it cum." It was the largest Italian sausage I had ever seen – especially on a man of such short stature. This hugest schlong totally shocked me! I nervously told him I had to leave and bolted out of the restaurant never to return.

Looking back on it, what was I thinking?!?!?! I should have stayed! But the evening wasn't a total loss. I left with the secret to making gnocchi that literally melts in your mouth.

Cheating Chris **ME!!!**

I have always been nice, friendly, social, and flirty. Chris was a friend of a friend who frequently came down to Los Angeles from Seattle for work. When my friend would have parties, I would talk with Chris and his wife, so I thought it was no biggie to meet up with him in L.A.

On one of these work trips, I made the mistake of not letting him drive back to his hotel because he was wasted. Seriously, I did not realize how he would interpret me taking him back to my place. I can be thick sometimes. My inner monologue is "I'm the happy-go-lucky girl next door. Men don't think of me like that." Well, he thought, "Of course, you want me. Who wouldn't?" Me! I don't do married AND I know your wife. Good gad. Stunk for me, too, because I was attracted to him.

He apologized. So, the next time he came to town I went out with him again. It wasn't awkward for me as I just chalked it up to those drunken moments and assumed that nothing further would happen because I established boundaries. And what does he do? He kissed me! My goodness.

So, I didn't see Chris again. I stopped going to parties at my friend's house. After a few years, I told her why and she was a bit surprised. When she eventually told her husband, he asked if I was sure Chris hit on me. Hmmm, a man shoving his tongue down my throat usually means something. I wasn't so clueless the second time around!

Teddy's Tryst   Me
Theater companies are generally full of drama that has nothing to do with the play. TDK Productions was no exception. I was cast as Nurse Ratched in "One Flew over the Cuckoo's Nest". So was Sally. This company always double cast their shows due to the high rate of dropouts. Teddy was the director and we developed a mutual interest in each other. We would sneak away after rehearsal to hang out and make out. I thought it was going somewhere.

The theater kept pushing back the show dates so Teddy finally said screw it and moved the production to another venue. Then he dropped me from the cast via email saying there was a conflict of interest. Really! I found out the conflict of interest was Sally, who was married, and they were getting it on. P.S. The show never opened!

Non-Smelling Nick   Him
Love of My Life #3
The next love of my life was younger. AWESOME! He just moved to L.A. = not yet tainted. EXTRA AWESOME!! And oh, curly hair, succulent lips, doe eyes, and a young face. A colt I really wanted in my corral. YEEHAW!

We met while I was volunteering at a film festival. He came over to find out what was going on. He asked me a few questions leading up to my number. For our first date, he took me to my favorite Chinese restaurant and ordered a bottle of expensive wine knowing my passion for it. He was indifferent to wine because he was born with no sense of smell. Afterwards, we went for a walk on the beach and played on the playground. Romantic, right? Yes, we did go back to his place and made out, and yes, it was pretty steamy. Best yet, garlic breath didn't matter!

The relationship went well for quite a while. At times, I felt I wasn't exactly what he wanted. Other times, I felt he wasn't exactly what I wanted. I was too outspoken and he smoked too much pot. (Theme here?) I know – he was younger. But I was patient. We had been dating for about six months when he threw me a wonderful surprise birthday party while his mom was in town. She was completely in on it. It was so sweet and I was really genuinely surprised! He wanted me to trust him and fall in love with him. So, I did. I thought we would get married. He even hinted at it. When my mom came to town, I took her to an open mic where Nick was going to debut the song he wrote for me. The song started with him telling me to open up and trust him, but then at the end the lyrics drastically changed with him telling me to slow down. Now wasn't that a mixed message?

I had been thinking about moving out of my studio apartment into a one-bedroom. He suggested we move in together. I suggested I buy a place and we move in there. (Insert record scratch as the needle is dragged across the vinyl.) He didn't like that idea at all. He wanted us to buy our first place together, and he wasn't ready to buy now. I thought he was being silly; we can gain equity, and why pay rent to someone else? This would work out great. He didn't agree.

We had been together for about 18 months. He knew it was time to shit or get off the pot. He jumped off the pot quite abruptly. I was shocked. Reflecting on this years later, I concluded our conflict was me wanting to buy a place and standing my ground and him feeling we were at different points in life and expecting stereotypical relationship roles.

He is now married to a woman who is my age and looks like me but isn't me. I found this out by Facebook friending his mom. I later unfriended her because I couldn't deal with it.

INTERNET DATING INTERMISSION PART 1

One at a time over the years, I tried eHarmony, Match, OKCupid, Plenty of Fish, and Chemistry.

While living in L.A., online dating sites became all the rage. Yes, you might make friends, but the chemistry isn't always there. There were too many dates to go through them all, so here are the highlights and lowlights. If you have never been on a dating site, it's all the men in a bar but multiplied by thousands. It's like shopping in a thrift store – you have to wade through a lot of crap before you find something decent. And then after a few wears, it falls apart.

Off Oscar **Me**

He was a pleasant online find. The first date was easy – dinner and drinks. He was fit, attractive, creating a new business, educated, conversational...and he looked like his picture, always an online dating bonus. But why oh why do men think it is okay to shove their tongue down your throat on the first kiss, particularly in a parking lot under a bright light? I was 13 again with Handy Hank sticking his hand up my shorts in the movie theater.

Well, I gave Oscar another chance. It was worth it – a nice holiday boat ride and a thoughtful gift of a book by an author I like. Even more important, he didn't shove his tongue down my throat at the end of the date. So, I decided to see where it might lead.

When I returned from a holiday vacation, we had a few dinners, movies, and some make-out sessions. He lived over an hour away which made it tough especially considering L.A. traffic.

One night, he thought it would be funny to put a Popsicle down my back. So not funny. I overreacted, but it became clear that he had this spark that seemed a little violent. I learned my lesson from Aussie Alex. It was time for me to leave. He was very, VERY upset, because he thought we had such chemistry. We broke up on the phone. I thought it was too far for either one of us to drive to actually break up in person and for my safety.

Tonsil Tommy   **Me**

Our first date was brunch. He chose a place that had a line that wrapped around the block. I commented how good the Bloody Marys and mimosas looked. He commented on drinking so early in the day was off-putting. He started getting touchy feely while we were waiting. Now I really needed a drink! We went for a long walk after breakfast. He stopped me in the parking lot and shoved his tongue down my throat. GROSS.

I believe in giving people the benefit of the doubt, in case you haven't already figured that out. Why was I so stupid again? He let me pay for the second date and tried to shove his tongue down my throat again. I fended him off.

Date three never happened. I had a busy week, so I told him I had to be home by 9pm. He said this was ridiculous and didn't think I really liked him that much. He wasn't feeling chemistry from me – that I was pulling away. I told him I didn't know him all that well and him shoving his tongue down my throat on the first date was a turn-off and inappropriate. He responded with – "LADIES LIKE IT!! Just in case you didn't know." I just about died. I told him "Take a poll, because most of the 'ladies' I know don't." He canceled our date. I was not the least bit disappointed.

Bad Breath Barry   **Me**

Barry had just bought an old Victorian house with his brothers and they were restoring it. I thought that was pretty cool. We had three dates. 1. Dinner. 2. Bike ride. 3. Movies. The attraction wasn't quite there. I mean, he was tall, lanky, and had curly hair. Usually a typical attraction for me. Except he was more appealing in his online pictures than in person. But he was nice and there was potential for growth. However, during the first two dates his breath was a little off, so the "no kiss" on his part was not a bad thing.

On the third date, after the movie, I went to the bathroom. When I walked out, he was waiting for me on the window ledge. He grabbed me and kissed me. Really? First kiss and you want it to be outside the women's bathroom? Plus... his breath was still off.

There was no fourth date. Barry was a nice guy but there was no chemistry on my part – and the bad breath...

Men who didn't seal the deal

Ginger Guy: 44-y/o man-Alta Dena-seeking women 30-45.

Picking up the messaging after some brief niceties...

> Sept 7
> Ginger Guy: I hope you are having a nice weekend.
>
> Me: I did. Thx. Hope you did as well. I have a funeral to go to on Wed in the OC. I won't be in Hollywood until early afternoon and work until 4. Could that work with your schedule? Let me know. Thanks.
>
> Ginger Guy: I'm sorry for the funeral you have to attend. I hope the person wasn't a very close person

to you. Later in the day could pose many problems. Rush hour traffic and I need to get to sleep by 5pm to get to work that evening. Another time?

Sept 9
Subject: Another time
Me: Let's reschedule. Give me some options.

Ginger Guy: Well, I'm awake and at home from 9 am to 4 pm daily. Weekends I'm typically free, although I may be canoeing in Newport Saturday. The week following I'll be attending a play that a good friend is directing. I don't like to drive out of my city on workdays because it drains my energy level, and I would like to stay on my gym schedule weekdays as well. I need to know your free times, and maybe we can work something out. Call me in the morning :)

Let's take a moment to reflect on that last text. Class, what have you learned about this individual so far?

1. Very structured person
2. Unable to deviate from routine
3. Can only do one thing at a time
4. Everything must fit into HIS schedule

Sept 11
Subject: Re: Re: Another time
Me: Friday night I will be up in that area but have a commitment from 7pm on. If I get out of work earlier I can give you a call and we could meet for a coffee in Burbank. Play it by ear? Or Sat I'm free after 7pm. I'll be up in NoHo. Sunday I'm free but it's your mom's day. Wednesday I may be free during the day. Otherwise we are looking at next

weekend. I guess it does seem that I am a bit unavailable but I do have free time weekday nights but that doesn't work for you.

Ginger Guy: If you want to meet in Alta Dena on Friday afternoon I might be up for that. I'm going out with friends in the evening and heading to Santa Barbara Saturday. What do you think? Sunday I have my mom as usual. During the week is a lot more difficult and I don't like to leave town on a work night. What do you think? Friday?

Sept 13
Re: Re: RE: Re: Another time
Me: Sorry. Just got the message now. Hope you are having a good time in Santa Barbara.

Ginger Guy: Thank you! It is a lot of fun.

Me: I really did want to meet you but it seems as like our available times don't match.

Ginger Guy: Well… I'm available but you are not willing to drive to Alta Dena.

Asshole alert!!! When has he ever offered to drive anywhere to meet me?? If he had ever looked at a map for a compromised meeting location, he would know that Alta Dena is one word "Altadena".

Me: I've compromised with Burbank and NoHo. There have been some glitches on both parts. I had a funeral. You canceled Fri for some reason. Women like to be pursued. Men will pursue if they're interested. It's hard – you work graveyard shift and I work typical business hours but if you were truly interested, you would make it happen without me having to come to your exact city.

Ginger Guy: After I meet you, then I'll start chasing you vigorously!!

Sept 14
Subject: You make it happen
Me: You would have to make the complete effort.

Ginger Guy: It will have to wait until week after next because I have a play next Saturday!!

Me: I am out of town that weekend.

Ginger Guy: We'll figure it out. Are you ever up here again soon?

Me: Why does it matter if I am up that way? If you want to make it happen, find a time that works for you to come to Huntington Beach and meet me. That is what the previous messages were about.

Ginger Guy: Well, I plan on going to Huntington Beach in a couple weeks, so I'll plan on calling you then. I have plans with friends on weekends until then. I don't have time for any dating really. But I am interested in you. Don't think I'm not!

Me: I disagree. I won't bore you with the details... just good luck with all sincerity.

PhD: 52-y/o man-Mid-Wilshire-seeking female companion 30-45.

PhD and I messaged back and forth for a few weeks. Scheduled a date. The morning of the date he messages:

> I must tell you that you are one of the two women I like the most. I just need some time. The problem is that I haven't had a relationship in years because even though my ex and I were divorced for 8 years, I still lived with her and my daughter until recently. We had our own separate rooms and we wanted our daughter to grow up with both a mom and a dad. She is 18 now and left for college a few weeks ago with her mother.
>
> I feel a freedom that I haven't had in years. As a man, I must tell you that I feel hungry. That's a poor choice of words, but I think you'd understand. I'm concerned that if you and I start seeing each other, we might break up just for that reason, and I don't want that to take that chance just in case.
>
> I hope you'll still be available in six months. I really would like to write to you then. I have your number but I don't have your email address in case you decide to leave this site. My email address is …

At this point, I decided online dating wasn't working for me. Everyone kept telling me I'm too picky. And they told me I put up with too much crap. It's a thing people like to tell single people as to why they are not in a relationship. Picky or not, I went back to the old-fashioned way: meeting men in a bar, at a coffee shop, through friends, at the gym…

RETURNING TO THE REST OF MY 30s
Meek-Turned-Mean Matt   Him

I met Matt at a friend's wedding. He was an average-looking shy guy, but there was something about me that made him break out of his shell. To many of his friends' amazement, Matt did a body shot off me, which to me was no big deal but to him was like "Oh my!!!!!"

He was about 10 years younger than me, but much younger than that socially and emotionally. However, he was really a smart guy. We met for dinner with Jackie when I was back up in Seattle. Once again, sweet, meek and nice, but not the bad boy I guess I was looking for at the time. I think he needed to catch up a bit so he wasn't so socially awkward.

Let's fast-forward about six years. I was back up in the Seattle area and included Matt in a group dinner with friends. It was nice to see him. He walked me back to my hotel and he grabbed my hand. We walked and talked for about a half hour or so. I invited him up to the hotel and he declined but gave me a sweet kiss.

We emailed more often after that and he decided to come down to L.A. for a visit. He seriously drove down on Friday and left on Monday. We went to my friend's play and then back to my house. We made out all night, took a walk on the beach in the morning, and decided to try the long-distance dating thing. Tuesday morning, I receive an email saying he changed his mind. He stated he was not comfortable getting into a relationship after his last break-up for "the reason" he didn't want to discuss. That is why he didn't go back to the hotel room with me and why he was having second thoughts about us dating.

We remained friends and emailed. He came down again to go camping in Big Bear. We slept in the same tent and ended up making out. We left early due to a big rainstorm passing through and went back to my place in the middle of the night. He slept in my bed and we made out.

I was getting mixed messages especially when Matt invited me up to Seattle for the weekend. We went to Mount Rainier and wine tasting in Woodinville. We talked but there was silence. We listened to music. It was a lovely day. On the last night, we went out to dinner with his roommate and the roommate's girlfriend. She was saying these horribly rude things about vegetarians and teachers. Well, I am both a vegetarian and a former teacher, of which she was well aware. It was miserable. The whole dinner conversation was not light, not friendly, and Matt didn't have my back at all. I was ready to leave. One more day. Ugh. So, the next morning, while lying in the same bed together where we have been making out for the last two nights, he told me that we would just always be friends because he doesn't feel like we have enough in common to date. Also, there were times when we were together that we didn't talk, and that made him uncomfortable. Plus, there was "the reason" which he gave prior for not wanting to date.

After he dropped me off at the airport, my flight was delayed a few hours. He lived close by, so I thought for a millisecond that I could call him. I decided not to because that would be more painful than waiting in the airport. I wasn't hurt by any of this, just truly shocked at the cluelessness and rudeness of the whole weekend. Why invite me to be your guest if you are going to treat me like shit? I was so over this meek-turned-mean man. Another LA/Seattle long distance relationship bites the dust.

Creepy Crawly Crawford   **Me**

I meet Crawford at a bar while out with a friend. He seemed okay. For the first date we met at the beach for a walk. He was half an hour late "because of traffic." He's an L.A. native and doesn't know there is usually traffic on the two-mile route he chose? I had just moved here and already knew that. He "claimed" he lived in his parents' former house with his sister and his pug. He kind of looked like a pug.

The turn-offs started on date three when he asked to come in and use my bathroom, which seemed reasonable. Once he got inside, he decided that he was "too" tired/drunk to drive home. I couldn't have an accident on my conscience. Pre-smartphone app taxi services. He stayed. Nothing happened, but I still felt played.

The next day he called and asked me where I saw this going. I said, "I don't know. As you already know, I'm dating other people." He got really upset – talking faster and raising his voice. He wanted us to be exclusive and I didn't want that at that point. I wasn't that into him and I felt I didn't know enough about him. During our next two dates, he kept dropping comments about "the other guy."

For someone who wanted something serious, he never invited me to his house. When I commented on that, his response was, "My mom still stops by whenever she wants... my sister is there..." Complete bullshit. Sounds like a married line to me. Every time he called or texted, I felt more and more repulsed. I ended it. It sounds like it went on forever, but it was less than six weeks.

Communication-less Clancy Both

I met Clancy at a wine tasting event, where I was networking the room for more clients for my consulting business. He called me and we chatted it up. We texted over the next few weeks. One morning he called and said he was in the area and wanted to take me to lunch. He had found a vegan restaurant that he wanted to try. I thought, "Wow, sweet and thoughtful!"

The Super Bowl was in a few days so we made a bet the loser would buy lunch next time. I won, so he brought lunch to our second date – picking up our wine shipment from a local winery we both belonged to. It was a fun date. He was charming and witty, plus there was definitely a steamy chemistry between us… literally! We fogged up the windows making out in the car. The third date was snowshoeing. I kicked his ass, especially uphill. We continued to casually date for the next few months – typical dinner, movies etc. This suited him fine. After all, he was getting the milk for free, so why buy the cow?

Initially that was fine for me, until I wanted to take it to the next level. That was when I discovered he was more into texting than talking. When I communicated that with him, his response was "Texting is best because I can answer at work." Guess what? He never responded at work. Hmmmm, maybe it wasn't a communication issue, maybe he just wasn't interested…

The last straw was when we had plans for a Friday night. He said to text him to let him know what time I would be done with my friends. I texted around 2pm to say I'd be done around 8pm. No response. I texted again around 8pm. He said he got off work early and went home to bed. Douchebag. We never texted again.

Insane Ira   Me

I met this one at a charity event. He seemed a little quirky, thought it might have been the vodka they were doling out. I was doing my networking thing and handed him my card.

We chatted a few times via phone, email, and text. Our first date was dinner, dessert, a play, and a short walk. It was nice… except that during dinner his eyes were darting everywhere. I wasn't sure if it was me (ha-ha) or ADHD. On the walk, he asked if he could give me a kiss. I thought "Oh, that's sweet." So, he did, a small one and then we parted.

He canceled the next date because his son had to stay with him later than he was supposed to. He asked if I was available that night. I already had plans, so no. He was annoyed. Seriously? Who canceled?

We tried to coordinate another date, but I had a very busy couple of weeks. So, I emailed him the six-time frames I had available over the next two weeks. He chose the last one. But since he waited three days to get back to me, I had already made plans. I don't keep my life on hold for people who can't get their life in order.

He called to tell me I'm difficult to date because it requires being available. I countered that it is unfair to place all the unavailability on me since he has his son most weekends, he waited three days to respond, and HE was the one who canceled our last date. He said touché and acquiesced.

Yes, after this there should not be another date. I know, I've said this before. However, we did come up with another day to have dinner. He chose the time and the place. He was late because he had to "run some errands."

Reasons I Should Have Become A Nun

The restaurant was one of these places where you pay at the counter and they bring the food to your table. I suggest splitting a pizza. He says, "Get your own, you can have it for lunch." As I am placing my order, he says, "You don't mind paying for your half this time?" Actually, I don't mind if it is understood from the get-go and not when I am at the counter and I had just offered to split the pizza. And yes, I should have left, but I only stayed for the pizza, sangria, and to avoid the L.A. rush hour traffic.

He went to the bathroom. I texted a friend "He made me pay for my own dinner!" When he came back, he asked about my new Smartphone and as I showed it to him, across the top comes the return text saying, "No third date!"

During dinner he invited me back to his place. I declined. The server came and asked if we wanted anything else. Yes, I know I missed another opportunity to leave but I wasn't about to miss the best warm chocolate chip cookie covered in soft-serve ice cream topped with luscious caramel and chocolate. Oh, and another sangria to make this last date more entertaining. The server asked if he should bring the drinks with the dessert. Ira said separate. I said together. No need to prolong this agony.

As I savored my dessert, he told me about how he cleaned his place before our last date and bought a new mattress pad cover. He wanted me to help put it on the bed. Gross! HELLO?? You want me to put out and you couldn't even buy me a $20 dinner?

Wait, there's more. The waiter came with the check for the dessert and two sangrias, I pulled out my card to split – he sits there. I paid. As I was walked to the bathroom before the drive home, he "whispered" from 12 feet across the restaurant, "Are you putting in a secret contraceptive?" I hoped he would have been gone when I got back. No such luck. Alas, he walked me to my car. No kiss to end this one because there wasn't going to be another date. But it wasn't a total waste. I got my pizza, sangria, warm ice cream cookie dessert, and avoided L.A. rush hour traffic.

Babyface Brett   Him
Maybe I read the signals wrong. It may have been gleeful anticipation of a younger man's attention. We met on a film shoot. He reached out to me on Facebook and started a chat with me and told me he's interested in women my age. He flirted with me on the set to the point where his friends started teasing him about it. He invited me to his summer party, so it seemed to me he was definitely interested since it was a personal invitation and not part of a group invite.

Not sure if he wanted to get the MILF thing on, or actually date. It didn't really matter at that point because he was just oh so cute. I showed up at the party 30 minutes late and was still the first to arrive. Finally, others started showing up and I had fun. When I was getting ready to go, he told me he didn't expect me to show up at the party and that his flirtiness is just part of his personality and sorry if he misled me. Ooops, did I read the signals wrong... or was he just chicken shit?

Fifty F-asshole Frank   Mutual
I generally date younger but that wasn't working too well, so what the heck. We met at an entertainment industry networking group. He was a speaker, actively working as a writer, director, and producer. I thought he could be a

good contact. We would meet once every few months for drinks when he was in town. He traveled around for his writing. He had places in L.A. and Orange County.

He invited me to go wine tasting in Temecula. It was a fun day! Towards the end, I was a little tipsy. I figured why not, so I decided to make out with him. Afterwards, we started seeing each other more regularly. He took me to Mexico for a weekend and always paid. It was nice. He opened doors. He was a little quirky, but aren't we all?

After about three months of that, I decided that I wasn't interested because it really wasn't developing into a relationship and I didn't like him enough for one anyway. DONE. It was convenient as he was off filming, so we didn't see each other for a while. When he came back, we were friends in my book. However, I never made it clear to him that we were strictly just friends again.

We would meet up occasionally for drinks so I could listen to him verbally masturbate about himself and the work he was doing. Nothing physical. I just wanted to keep his connection to the industry open.

One night he was in town and wanted to meet up. Maggie was visiting from Seattle so I told him it would be both of us. He said okay. Normally the conversations were all about him, which I was fine with because I really didn't want to talk much about myself. Maggie and I hadn't seen each other for a while so we dominated the conversation, but even when I tried to draw him in, he would not engage. He finally pulled out work to do. She asked, "Are we boring you?" He said, "Kind of." She threw $10 on the table for her drink and says, "Fine, we're leaving." I was dumbfounded. I said, "I have to go. Sorry. We'll talk later." And left without putting any money down.

Well, for him "talking later" meant sending me a text. "Soooooo much fun with you and your friend." I responded, "You're an ass:)" He said, "You're a cunt and your friend is too. Fuck off, really." I responded, "I was just being sarcastic back." I deleted him from Facebook and my phone.

About a month later I received an email requesting to remove him from my newsletter list. Dumb shit could just unsubscribe himself. I am so glad he made the extra effort to let me know he really did mean "Fuck off, REALLY." Ha!

Magic Mike – 29 Going On 2   Him, Me

We had a quick first date over a drink. He was younger but what the heck, I dig the youngin's. He wanted to kiss in the bar but I'm not a PDA (Public Display of Affection) kind of girl. We were going to go for a walk but he was skeptical about leaving his car. I just went home.

On date two, I met him at his house on my way back from work because it was easier for me. He suggested this old-school throwback restaurant with red leather booths, dark wood floors, and wrought-iron fixtures. You could sense what it was like back in the 1950s and '60s – smoke-filled, serving scotch on the rocks and martinis. The kitschiness was so up my alley. We waited for a table to order drinks and appetizers. The waitress told us we had to move to the bar because tables were for dinner only. Annoyed that we should have been told before waiting, we left and went for sushi. He ate with his fingers, wolfed down his food, and reflecting back on the date, was impatient while I finished mine. We went for ice cream and walked back to his place. We started fooling around, then he felt sick and asked me to leave. He never called. I never called. Thank God. Another bullet dodged.

Fast forward two years, and I get a phone call at 11 pm. He said, "It's Mike from Match, we had a few dates a couple years ago. Do you remember me?" My response was a simple "No." Okay, I did, but I wanted to hear him explain the situation. He went on to tell me he was 31 now. I said I had to go to bed. He asked if I turned into a pumpkin. I said yes. Two weeks later he texts me.

(714) KID-DATE: Sup Mary Katharine

Me: Who is this?

(714) KID-DATE: Michael from match. Called u a few weeks ago. We had sex December '09

Me: Kind of. If I recall you freaked out, asked me to leave because "you felt sick" all of a sudden and then called me 2 years later to say "hey". Thank you for thinking of me but I'm not interested.

(714) KID-DATE: I had stomach cramps. Sue me. Don't u want my hot body? I want to fuck right this time.

Me: But my time is too precious for a two-year overdue call. I have other options in getting the job done right time & time again.

(714) KID-DATE: U on Facebook.

Me: Ur kidding.

He calls. I don't answer.

(714) KID-DATE: You won't answer. Youre weak. I was going to tell you why I didn't call.

Me: Text it or leave a vm.

(714) KID-DATE: Call me.

(714) KID-DATE: You don't want my huge cock again? I'm In LA tonight.

(714) KID-DATE: I give up

Did I ever talk to him to find out the "why?" Yes, I did. He told me, in not so many words, he didn't want another date initially because I believed in embracing my natural feminine body and he wasn't used to that. (Thank you, porn, landing strips, and Brazil for creating the warped sense of what a "woman's body" should be... especially in SoCal!) However, now he could accept it. Too late!

Hot Carl   Me

Carl and I met in acting class. He was beautiful! His skin was the color of a mocha latte with freckles and loosely curled hair. I invited him to a party at my apartment. He showed up, stayed after and we made out. I invited him again a few weeks later. He showed up again. He stayed after again along with my friend Zaney. Carl told us some stories that went from unusual to very weird. He mentioned that his last girlfriend made him poop on a glass table while she watched underneath. I don't know what was more disturbing: the fact that he went out with someone who would suggest that or that he actually did it! He looked like some fine milk chocolate but I didn't want to see it coming out of his ass! He followed this with a request for a threesome. The evening ended abruptly and thankfully I never saw or heard from Carl again!

40 AND FABULOUS!

As much as I loved my West Coast life, I wanted to move back east. I was a city gal at heart and what place better to settle than New York. I had only dated West Coast men. Now was my chance to see how East Coast men differ. Let's find out! In my forties, George Clooney suddenly became very good looking. He aged very well and had become more attractive with time.

Wanker Willie   **Me**

I had only been in the city a month when I was walking down the street and this guy saw me and started walking with me. He asked me out on a date and I thought as long as it was in a public place, why not?

We met a few days later at a beer and burger bar. He went on and on about how smart, rich, and important he and his entire family were. And he had this buddy and that buddy and so on and so on. What a blowhard! I don't think I said a word. I couldn't wait to leave. And I learned a lesson from all the dates before to just finish the entrée with no dessert nor second drink.

As we were walking towards our individual destinations, he became another one who thought a deep passionate kiss consisted of shoving his tongue down my throat on the first date. I gave no signs of "kiss me now" because as I mentioned, I couldn't leave fast enough – plus, I was expecting a phone call. And as I was walking home, Perfect Pete (see below) called. Willie did text me for another date. I said no. Am I finally learning to say no sooner?????

Perfect Pete   Him
Summer lovin', had me a blast... Summer dreams, ripped at the seams

It was a quick romance, but oh so complete. We met at a fun bar where you play games, drink beer, and eat candy bars. My friend and I were playing Scrabble, and I chatted up the guys sitting next to us. No intentions, just being my friendly self. As they were leaving, one of the guys asked me for my number. I thought why not and I gave it to him. It wasn't me networking and giving my card. He asked! WOOHOO! AND he called! A man with follow-through. DOUBLE WOOHOO! AND it was on the night of the horrible date with Wanker Willies. TRIPLE WOOHOO!

I was smitten from that first phone call. Pete told me how to fix the flat tire on my bicycle since I had never changed the rear tire with gears. After the call, I changed his name in my phone to MHTB (My Husband to Be) to put into the universe what I wanted. Too soon? My first time doing something like that.

The first date was on a warm Saturday night. Remembering I was a tequila aficionado from the first conversation at the fun bar, he took me to a tequila bar. When I walked in and saw him, I was gone, completely melted on the floor. I didn't quite remember what he looked like from our first meeting since the bar was dark but he was remarkably cute, having all the features I love. Great locks of hair and huge eyes and an amazing smile. On a side note, a friend saw his picture and said, "He's cute except for his hair and eyes." HAHAHAHAHA. It was a 12-hour first date. We talked for over eight hours before a kiss even landed. We spent the night cuddling and kissing and went for breakfast together the next morning. It was like 4 dates in one.

Over the next few days, he texted me sweet nothings and pictures of food, his motorcycle, cocktails, and sunsets. He was instigating it. I was taking the back seat.

By the end of the week, I received a text: "Not ready for a relationship." I said "One date does not a relationship make. We're just getting to know each other." He decided to accept my logic and asked me on another date.

Pete didn't miss a beat with continuing to text me. I was cautious to make sure he was initiating it, not me, and texting just enough not to scare him off. He sent me more pictures of cocktails and dinners he made, and the process of changing the oil in his car. These are characteristics I want in a man – good in the kitchen AND willing to get his hands dirty.

The fifth date, I mean second date was a few weeks later. I suggested a gallery opening for a photographer friend (Pete's also a photographer) and then go to listen to some music at Lincoln Center as part of their summer festival. The gallery exhibit had candid portraits of well-known bands. We had a fantastic time. He initiated all physical contact including hand holding, sitting close to me, and kissing me that afternoon.

I told him earlier I was meeting a friend at Penn Station who was going to be staying with me. He wanted to join us for dinner which was fine with us. I tend to be a bit forward, or as my friends put it "emasculating". But I was trying my best not to be that way because I really, really liked him. So at dinner, I slid the wine menu to him for him to order. He snickered and passed it back to me because and stated, "You know more about wines than I do." My heart fluttered a little more. All through dinner we were playing footsie. I didn't think my friend knew, but I'm sure she did.

As we walked back to my place from dinner, I carried my friend's bag. He realized that and took it from me. After a while, he was futzing with the bag and I asked if he wanted me to take it for a bit – just being nice because that is who I am. Then the little voices of my friends were in my head saying "Emasculating! Emasculating!"

When we got back to my place, it was time to say goodbye. My friend went upstairs and I said I'll be there in a bit. She winked at me. Talk about a "Sex in the City" moment. We were in front of my apartment building, he grabbed me in a gentle yet forceful way and planted the best romantic novel kiss on me. It topped New Year's Nate's midnight kiss by leaps and bounds. It remains one of the most amazing good night kisses in my life.

Amid making out, I apologized for offering to take the bag. I said "I'm not too good at this dating thing. I don't play games. I only know how to be me, and my friends tell me it comes across as emasculating." He grabbed me, kissed me, and said, "How can I feel emasculated? Whenever I touch you and kiss you, I can feel you melt in my arms!" And he was absolutely right. I melted all over that stoop.

Date three we went to an outdoor concert near my house. I was late coming home from work and rode my bike. I met him at the door. I was a hot mess and not in a good way. I was so mad at the people at work. I was all ready to leave and was asked to do ONE MORE THING, which made me late. GGGRRRRRR.

While I took a shower, he kindly put the picnic basket together with the ingredients I had but no time to arrange them. We went and enjoyed our picnic outside the concert area but couldn't take the leftovers in.

We walked back to my house to drop the stuff off and started making out. I knew where this was heading and I was trying to be good – although I didn't want to be. So, we got up and we went back to listen to the music. We absolutely hated the music and came back after about 45 minutes. There was more kissing and cuddling and me refraining from going too far. He did stay over and the next morning I sent him off with some coffee for his drive into work in my favorite coffee mug.

We texted all weekend because I had family in town and was unavailable to meet up. On Tuesday, I received the "Thanks but no thanks" text, a month after the first one. He was nice, stating that he liked me and knows that I appreciate honesty. He only saw this going towards a relationship and that was not what he wanted at the moment. He thought he could do the casual dating thing but could not. I wish I had saved the text, but I was so crushed. I deleted it. I responded with "Thank you for the honesty and if you change your mind and want a relationship, get in touch with me." Then I cried for a while.

I reached out to him a few times throughout the next year with invites to gallery openings and other things I knew would be of interest to him, in order to keep me in his mind. Yeah, I know. If he were interested, he would have contacted me regardless. It took a while to delete the emails. I re-read them and man, they were from two people obviously into one another. I just don't get it... And I didn't get the coffee mug back either.

I knew that was the chance I was taking after the first time he played the "I don't want a relationship" card. I was thinking of two dear friends of mine who played it cool, not rushing men they were dating, and the fact that they have been happily married for ten-plus years now. I also thought I was not rushing anything and just letting it happen.

I know it was only three dates, but I was hit hard. I mistook his very flirty, friendly texts and dates to be more than they were, as any person head-over-heels would have. I honestly thought he was the one.

I had just moved to NYC and believed that things would come together here. I had wanted to move here for a few years. I believed it was my time after all the hard work and struggles I had put in with dating and career choices. I haven't yet felt the same way about any of the dates I have gone on since.

Amorous Art   Neither

While at a rooftop bar with some friends, this random girl joined us. The rest of her friends came over. I started talking to the only male in the group. He was new to New York. He asked for my number. He called and we met for a drink. On the date, he made a reference to the TV show "Dawson's Creek". Mind you, I like the young ones but then I realized he was really, REALLY young.

So, I asked – "How old are you?"

He answered, "How old are you?"

"I asked you first."

"27. And you?"

"You have to guess."

"Won't play that game, got me into trouble before."

"It'll be like 21 questions. If you don't guess, I'll tell."

"Early 30s?" I shook my head no.

"37. The same age as my older sister."

"No."

The conversation continued and we talked about one of my favorite movies, "Star Wars." I mentioned that my grandpa took me to see it when it first came out. As we left the bar, he says "42." I was so insulted that I responded with a "NO!" Then, after a pause: "Wait, yes, later this year" and then I laughed.

We went to a few more spots; he paid for the whole night. I offered to help pay. He said "No, I asked you on the date." Older guys should take a lesson from this youngin'. It developed into a very steamy night. There is a reason why women in their 40s and men in their 20s work well together. Although we tried to have subsequent dates, it just didn't happen with our schedules. Oh well.

INTERNET DATING INTERMISSION PART 2

How much did Internet dating change over ten years? Is it different in NYC than L.A.? Are there new sites to try? What about the sites that have been around for a while? I retried eHarmony, Match, OKCupid and then some new ones – How About We, Bumble, and Coffee Meets Bagel.

King of Queens? I Think Not   Me

My first mistake (for this date, anyway) went to the guy instead of the guy coming to me. He said he would normally drive to meet me, but due to Hurricane Sandy it was challenging to get from Queens to Manhattan because of road and bridge closures. But then he said he doesn't ride the subway. I don't care if you live in Queens, you should know how to ride the subway in New York!! So, I met him at the Queens subway station. He did not look at all like his picture and he took me for coffee at... Dunkin' Donuts. I rode the subway all the way to Queens to a Dunkin' Donuts AND he didn't even offer me a donut!

I quickly discovered I wasn't interested. We talked about movies and TV shows that we liked, and he suggested we go to his place and watch South Park. I said no. We talked some more and he asked me to go to his place again. I said no. Then he asked if I wanted to go for a ride in his car. Again, I said no. Then he tried to give me a good night kiss on the lips. I turned my head and backed up so the kiss landed on the cheek. I disappeared down into the subway and headed home. Obviously, no second date.

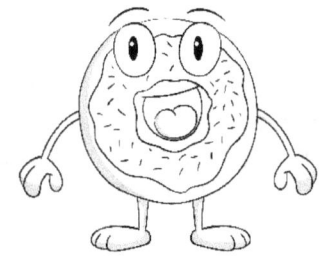

Puppet "Man"uel   Neither

First red flag should have been his profile picture. He was holding a puppet, and I noticed the puppet was cuter. But I was intrigued. We chatted and he said he enjoyed the conversation enough to go out on a date.

Now, I always like to have the guy choose the place for a date because it says a lot about him. He chose some lame Mexican/Irish place with a happy hour. When met there, he stated, "Only drinks on the first date." At least he didn't make me order the happy hour drinks.

He was the owner of a small production company in the entertainment industry. I told him about my bad experiences pursuing acting in L.A. He suggested I go into casting. I mentioned that there are many bitter ex-actors who do it. He said I would fit right in. NICE.

Apparently, he had a 90-minute rule for first dates, as he abruptly said he had to leave. Outside he gave me the complete pat-on-the-back hug, turned his face for the "I don't want to give any indication that I want to kiss her," and stated he had a "nice time". He was sooooooo not interested and could care less.

A couple of weeks later, I was at my friend Colleen's house for dinner. I told her about the guy and what he did for a living. She asked me if his name is Manuel. I say yes. She cracked up. He was an ex of hers from a few years ago. Small world even in New York.

Okay, here is a complete ass moment on my part. I sent him a message through the dating site, saying "Colleen says hi." He responded back with "Small world." He was never going to contact either one of us, and he was a bit of an arrogant weenie anyway.

Sweet Sweaty Squeaky Sam   Me

We met on How About We. He was average-looking, had a good job, a good relationship with his family, liked to travel, and sounded adventurous. On paper, a good catch.

We had only emailed and texted before our first date. He picked a rooftop bar overlooking Manhattan. It was quite a shock when he opened his mouth and he sounded exactly like Fran Drescher from "The Nanny," with a high-pitched Queens accent. Within the first hour, I knew when he moved out of his parents' house, how much money he made, his exes, his career moves, where he has travelled to, and where he wants to go. I managed to adjust to his voice, and I found that he was a genuinely nice guy and we had a lot of common interests. So okay, there would be a date two.

He got us tickets for Shakespeare in the Park. He picked up dinner and macaroons for dessert. We had a pleasant time, except it was a bit hot and muggy. He was a bit of a "sweater" and kept wiping his face in his t-shirt sleeve. Ohh noooo. If you know you are going to sweat, bring something to wipe your face.

He walked me to the subway station. He zeroed in for what I thought was a kiss. So, I kissed him. For him it was just supposed to be a hug. I misread the signals, again. He seemed a bit freaked out. Not sure why. So okay, onto date three.

We met at a nice Mexican restaurant because he knew I liked tequila. He looked nice but he was wearing a long-sleeved shirt on a hot day. This time at least he brought a handkerchief. Progress!! Dinner was nice, but after several self-deprecating comments, I got annoyed and told him to cut it out. It wasn't a nice thing to do but I couldn't take it anymore. I offered to pay the check and he refused saying, "I just better get another date out of this!"

By the time we walked to the subway, his shirt was drenched with sweat. I knew he couldn't help it, but it was just too much. Then he asked the magic question, "Where is this going? I don't want to waste my time." I responded, "I don't know. We are dating and getting to know each other." Later that evening, I ended it by text, having realized it is just a good way to go sometimes.

> Me: Sam, I've been thinking about what you said about not wasting your time if this was not going anywhere. I enjoyed our conversations, the well thought out & planned dates. You are sincere & sweet. In the long run, I don't think we are a good match in the dating sense. I wish you the best on your search for a mate. If you want a hiking companion, let me know:-) Thanks for all you did.

> (718) MEH-DATE: Hi MK, Thank you for your honesty. I think you are a very thoughtful and compassionate person. Best of luck in your NYC Triathlon and your search for someone special. Sam

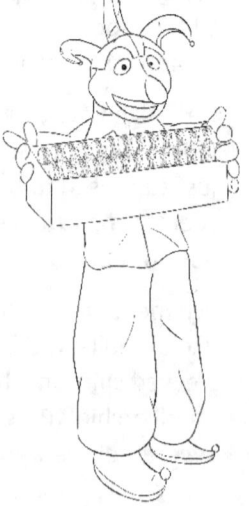

He was great on paper, but the chemistry just wasn't there.

Getting Stood Up Two Times in One Week
Guy 1 – Horny Harold   Him

I met Harold on one of the free Internet dating sites. I wasn't really interested. He didn't meet my checklist of items regarding physical appeal and he lived way out in Queens. Learned my lesson there. But he was persistent, so I decided to give him a chance to see if his personal charm could sway me.

He continued to show interest over the next week. He asked me out. He picked a dive bar. I like dive bars. On the day of the "date," he sent me the following text:

> Feb. 10 – 11:20 a.m.
> (347) BAD-DATE: Rudy's...44th n 9th Ave.
>
> Me: Sure...5.
>
> (347) BAD-DATE: U work close to there?
>
> Me: No but gives me enough time to get there.
>
> (347) BAD-DATE: ok so rudys five.

I went inside, looked around and didn't see him. Two guys started talking to me. I looked at my phone and saw this text sent at 4:55 p.m.:

> (347) BAD-DATE: i think i am too horny to see u..,i have not had sex in months, n would probably say something inappropriate.

I showed them the text. They were disgusted, or at least acted so. They bought me a beer. The joke was on me. I was the one stood up. He never showed. The guys couldn't believe he didn't show up either. Creep.

Guy 2 - Snowy Sid   **Him**

Same week, same free Internet dating app and same venturing outside of my "type" once again. So many of my friends married someone "not their type." So, Sid and I agreed to meet at a bar. I got there on time. I waited. I waited. I waited. All the while he texted me to let me know he is on the way.

>(646) BAD-DATE: Casa Lula? (5:11 p.m.)

>Me: need address or have it? (5:13 p.m.)

>(646) BAD-DATE: Stuck in some snow in my parking space....cleaning it out now n be there in 20 min (5:29 p.m.)

>(646) BAD-DATE: Car almost out. Can we do bocca actually? Sorry for the change but I know I find parking around there usually....it's like 54th n 55th on 9th ave. (5:30 p.m.)

>Me: Sure (5:30 p.m.)

>Me: I'm here (5:40 p.m.)

I ordered a glass of wine from a cute, friendly bartender.

>(646) BAD-DATE: Parking now... it's crazy with the snow (6:00 p.m.)

>Me: I'm leaving (6:15 p.m.)

The glass of wine was empty.

Getting Stood Up Two Times in One Week
Guy 1 – Horny Harold   Him

I met Harold on one of the free Internet dating sites. I wasn't really interested. He didn't meet my checklist of items regarding physical appeal and he lived way out in Queens. Learned my lesson there. But he was persistent, so I decided to give him a chance to see if his personal charm could sway me.

He continued to show interest over the next week. He asked me out. He picked a dive bar. I like dive bars. On the day of the "date," he sent me the following text:

> Feb. 10 – 11:20 a.m.
> (347) BAD-DATE: Rudy's...44th n 9th Ave.

> Me: Sure...5.

> (347) BAD-DATE: U work close to there?

> Me: No but gives me enough time to get there.

> (347) BAD-DATE: ok so rudys five.

I went inside, looked around and didn't see him. Two guys started talking to me. I looked at my phone and saw this text sent at 4:55 p.m.:

> (347) BAD-DATE: i think i am too horny to see u..,i have not had sex in months, n would probably say something inappropriate.

I showed them the text. They were disgusted, or at least acted so. They bought me a beer. The joke was on me. I was the one stood up. He never showed. The guys couldn't believe he didn't show up either. Creep.

Guy 2 - Snowy Sid   Him

Same week, same free Internet dating app and same venturing outside of my "type" once again. So many of my friends married someone "not their type." So, Sid and I agreed to meet at a bar. I got there on time. I waited. I waited. I waited. All the while he texted me to let me know he is on the way.

> (646) BAD-DATE: Casa Lula? (5:11 p.m.)

> Me: need address or have it? (5:13 p.m.)

> (646) BAD-DATE: Stuck in some snow in my parking space....cleaning it out now n be there in 20 min (5:29 p.m.)

> (646) BAD-DATE: Car almost out. Can we do bocca actually? Sorry for the change but I know I find parking around there usually....it's like 54th n 55th on 9th ave. (5:30 p.m.)

> Me: Sure (5:30 p.m.)

> Me: I'm here (5:40 p.m.)

I ordered a glass of wine from a cute, friendly bartender.

> (646) BAD-DATE: Parking now... it's crazy with the snow (6:00 p.m.)

> Me: I'm leaving (6:15 p.m.)

The glass of wine was empty.

Picking Peter   Me

I found him on Bumble. A swipe-right, swipe-left site where the woman makes the initial move. As a general rule, they need to have a bio section and more than one picture for me to swipe right. He had the bio, but I didn't look at <u>all</u> the pictures before swiping right. Pics holding giant fish or mirror selfies are generally swipe-lefts. I didn't see the mirror selfie before swiping right. Clue #1.

It escalated quickly from a texting conversation to him asking me on a date. I still want them to ask me out on the date, otherwise I'll steamroll the relationship, and I don't want to do that. I gave a list options and he chose from there, commenting on some future date places. So, we met at this interesting bar that had great old-school décor and looked like an old speakeasy. We had a couple of drinks and good conversation. He had some weird head twitching ticks. But it was a first date, so I let them go.

We talked and texted back and forth for the next two weeks. He asked for another date, and since the first date was fine, I agreed. He commented that I was playing with my hair on the first date and when he looked that up online it meant that I was nervous. I rarely get nervous on dates. I told him it was because I have a wall up.

Date two was from one of the places on the original list. When I arrived, he asked if it was okay to sit at the bar instead of a table. That was fine. He talked to me about some deal he got at work and kept on telling me how he was "so weird" and how his job was "so weird" and how he is "so different". I channeled Winnie-the-Pooh and wanted to exclaim "Oh, bother!" I thought "probably no third date". Then he said, "Watch, this is what I do," and started talking to the people next to us. They were polite and conversed with us. He was disappointed that they wanted to go to their own table for dinner instead of staying with us. He again said, "Wait, watch, this is what I do." He approached another couple and was offended when they didn't want to join us. So back to just the two of us. Then came the clincher for no third date.

It looked like his nose itched. First his finger rubbed under it. Then he started to rim the nostril. And then I turned away trying to figure out what to say, I noticed with my amazing peripheral vision that he went whole hog. His finger went in. DONE!!

Yes, I should have found a reason to leave, but I was not that quick in panic mode. I left a giant schlong but stayed for nose picker. What the heck! During the conversation, he kept hinting towards his ex-wife and I thought "Alright, he wants to talk about this, I'll ask a few questions." Peter got uncomfortable and started pacing in the bar. I changed the subject. As we were talking, HE DIGS IN AGAIN! I looked at him and asked, "Do you need me to see if the bartender has a napkin?" He said, "No. It's just a nervous tick." OMG! What will the next tick be, thumbing his butt or searching for belly button lint?

We finished the drinks and left. We walked a few blocks, fluctuating between him being with me or 20 feet ahead. I was like "whatever". He then came back and kissed me on the lips. It was a GROSS kiss! Right there with First Kiss and Diggity Doggity Dan. Yuck. I pulled away. I don't recall what he said because I was still astounded by his behavior and was just over the whole thing. I said goodbye and turned down my block. He walked to his train. The following texting thread ensued:

> (551) BAD-DATE: want to make out again? want to come over to Long Island for dinner? im not going to hurt you just enjoy your company. im on train

thinking about making out with you so you figure out something for next week

Next afternoon

Me: Thank you for the drinks last night. I wish you luck on your new chapter, I don't feel the same connection you seem to.

(551) BAD-DATE: what? really? what did i do to repel you?

Me: You didn't. Just not there for me. (Should have called him out on the nose picking.)

(551) BAD-DATE: i dont know what to say i could spend hours talking with you and spent hours thinking about you. so ok. later bye

Me: I'm sorry I do wish you happiness.

(551) BAD-DATE: i just dont understand. im really disappointed can we have 1 more date?

Me: I'm sorry you are disappointed. I understand how you feel as I have been in that position more times than I wish. Another date will not make a difference. There are many more wonderful women out there.

(551) BAD-DATE: Why not

Me: Because I don't want to. Good luck. (Again, should have called out the nose picking.)

(551) BAD-DATE: whatever close off someone who wanted to get past your wall good luck on your lonely journey

A lonely journey is better than a journey with the wrong person, especially a nose picker

Dirty Dog Rescuing Dillon   **Him, then Me**

Dillon and I met through eHarmony. I had recently invested in the paid site, again, hoping to find a real relationship. I made the crazy mistake of thinking he too was looking for something serious. He was smart, well educated, a pilot, about my age, and never married. This text exchange picks up after the first date...

May 1st – early morning

    (732) ODD-DATE - Good morning Mary; have an awesome day and I will see you soon :-)

    Me: You have a good day too. Rode my bike in today. Felt good.

    (732) ODD-DATE - I might be able to do tomorrow. I may have a cancellation I'll let you know.

    Me: OK. lose-win for you. boo on the cancellation but then you get to see me. the latter part was the win in case you missed it. :)

    (732) ODD-DATE - No, I got it ;-)

    Me: That's right. You are like me. You are quick witted, smarmy at times, and often sarcastic with a strong self-confidence.

    (732) ODD-DATE - Some might refer to it as a superiority complex. However if it's actual it's not a complex B-)

    Me: It just is... It's all in the tone you use whether it is strong self-confidence or superiority complex. One of those fine lines, Like the ones around my eyes.:/ I will check back with you later.

    (732) ODD-DATE - Have fun! I'll be hiking in the woods. Try to get out for lunch it's amazing outside!

Midafternoon...

> Me: Going for walk. Do you know about tomorrow? Have another invite but wanted to check with you first since we do have tentative plans.

> (732) ODD-DATE: YES

> Me: I feel tomorrow will be a bit of a long day at work. Who is going where?

> (732) ODD-DATE: I will have to figure that out later. I'm on my way to the airport :-)

Later that night...

> Me: I have a solution. I can take the ferry over to Jersey. I will not have bike so you can meet me at the ferry terminal and we can walk to wherever. Will you be bringing dinner? You can then drive me to the PATH train because it is easiest for me walk home from there. :)

> (732) ODD-DATE: Do you know how to get to the PATH from Liberty State Park?

> Me: That's what gps is for :)

> (732) ODD-DATE: Sweetie, I'm exhausted! I'm just going to go to bed. I'll talk to you in the morning :-) See what time the latest ferry is. PS, you don't strike me as a skirt kind of girl, I like them a lot! Since you're not on your bike in would you wear a skirt?

> Me: if you haven't noticed I don't like being told what to do nor be judged. :) and it really is funny because i wear skirts more than pants.

May 2nd– morning

(732) ODD-DATE: Well unlike you, I do like being told what to do. My personality is so dominant in the real world, I like being subservient sexually. Enjoy being degraded – pull my hair, spit on me - especially my face and mouth, gag me by sticking your fingers down my throat. I am a weirdo, BUT a reciprocating weirdo.;-) And it is amazing when you cum from doing that to me and that it truly turns you on and you are doing it for you as much as me, but just for me is awesome too! And PS I think you do like being told what to do as well

Me: Wow! By the way, I wasn't talking sexually. Interesting info to know. I don't do the degrading thing. Not part of my being at the core. I can't treat people that way intentionally even if it brings you pleasure. That doesn't dismiss some other items:-)

(732) ODD-DATE: That's ok, everyone has boundaries, comfort zone/level. I respect it all. I love dirty talk, not so much hearing it with regard to what I like but I love talking it. Our biggest sex organ is our brain. Hearing the right words can put me right over the top where I need to be. And the details of pulling hair a certain way, on a certain angle at a certain time can easily make a woman achieve orgasm even women who told me they have never had an orgasm before. When it comes to sex, I have become very learned. I create nuances of sex. Restrain me. Not handcuffs or ropes, with your hands. The arousal is pretending that I want you to stop but you don't.

This is just play. But it's a good thing to know prior about me because it does take me there ;-) If I start to complain, tell me to shut up. That is part of the play. I have been with women that never experienced being the dominant one and ended up really liking it and getting truly aroused by it I am well versed at reading and facilitating someone's sexual preferences and safe fantasies ;-) Ok going to get my things done to be able to see you tonight.

Me: I get what you are saying about the other stuff. And yes, it is our brain that decides so much about who we are, how we act, react, and feel. But there is something that isn't sitting right, not sure how to express it. Will mull it over while putting together this proposal at work and we can discuss when I get the words. Have a great day.

(732) ODD-DATE: It is perfectly okay. It takes a certain type of woman to like the kind of things that I like. Most women enjoy being dominated and not dominating. Although as I have expressed I can be anybody's fantasy, I'm very good at it! I put things out there immediately because I have been with a lot of women and I don't like playing the game of taking all the time trying to figure out if we're sexually compatible. That is exhausting. It's a waste of our times if it's not going to work and it doesn't seem like we are going to make a connection, so I hope the best for you :-)

Me: Are you saying we are not sexually compatible without even trying? We were having a dialogue, right? Communicating? Did I just miss a giant leap?

Over a month later... June 7th – morning

(732) ODD-DATE: I want to apologize for being such a flake. I just get agitated very easily because my career is not only stressful but rescuing animals in very volatile and dangerous situations puts me in fight mode at all times. I would hope that we can start over but if you do not want that I understand. I hope that you had an awesome Memorial Day and I truly do hope to talk to you soon - B-)

Me: Did you send this to right person?

(732) ODD-DATE: Yes I did. I see you're still a brat :-P

Me: I will forever be a brat. Thanks for apologizing although I don't think it is necessary. You weren't being a flake you were being honest with what you wanted. It could have been fun but in the end, I am not what you want. Albeit role-playing is a fun part of the experience, for me, I would want my long-term relationship to be more intimate and real. Good luck.

If there is one good thing about texting, people will write shit that they would never have the balls to say in person.

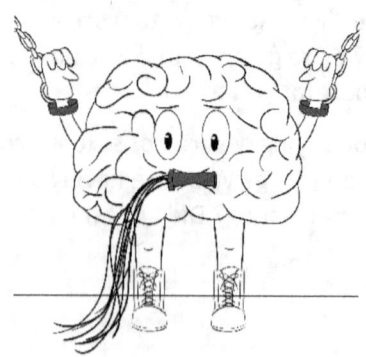

RETURNING TO THE REST OF MY 40s

Texting vs. Talking

I used to be a phone talker when I lived in L.A. and drove everywhere. Since I moved to New York, walking and biking are my means of transportation. It's impossible to have a conversation when you are out on the streets.

Texting can be a horrible way to communicate but it seems to be the norm now, and it's efficient and an easy way to make date. However, I would much rather meet these Internet dates to see if there is chemistry. With texts, you don't get the intonations, voice fluctuations, sarcasm, wit, or humor. It also gives people the opportunity to hide, do and say things or break up in ways they wouldn't if they had to do it in person or even over the phone as you will see in the stories ahead.

Unappealing Useless Ulysses   Me

Ulysses was staring at me from across the coffee shop and then stood in line behind me for the bathroom to strike up a conversation. He asked me out for coffee and I said sure. No one ever tried to pick me up while waiting for the bathroom before!

We met for coffee. He was late and I had to get back to work. After talking for 20 minutes, I knew there was no chemistry. But the next day, he started to text:

June 13th - 8:17 p.m. to 9:11 p.m.

> (928) BAD-DATE: Hey whats up? Wanted to check on you:)

> Me: Hi. Rehearsing the play. Thanks for checking in, I have a feeling you are young. How old are you?

(928) BAD-DATE: Ohhh this question again:) I could be younger than you but I like dating older woman.

Me: Doesn't answer my question.

(928) BAD-DATE: I don't want the age to be a problem from the start. I would rather tell you later if you don't mind:) Is it a deal breaker for you?

Me: I think it is.

(928) BAD-DATE: What is your age requirement? :)

Me: Still doesn't answer my question.

(928) BAD-DATE: I will tell you but why don't you get to know me first?

Me: I know we met only briefly but I'm not feeling a romantic connection.

I was hoping to use age as the reason for ending this. It's less harsh than no chemistry.

(928) BAD-DATE: Hmmm. You might feel different later. If you were not attracted to me and then you might have total different feelings than now. (Yes, this is what was typed) Honestly I don't have too much of a romantic feeling either but I think that is normal. We spent very little time together. However I think you are very beautiful.

(928) BAD-DATE: I am taking the actuarial exam on Saturday. Will finish after 4 and so can meet after if you want. Shall we? After this you can decide, ok?

I meant to respond but didn't. So, two days later...

June 15th - 3:28 p.m.

(928) BAD-DATE: Hey I am in Manhattan. Would you like to meet up?

Later this evening (9:50 p.m.) ... after not seeing the text, I courteously followed up with:

> Me: I hope your test went well. I wish you the best of luck on your future plans. I went out with you because I appreciated the fact that you came & asked. I am sorry I'm just not interested.

> (928) BAD-DATE: Oh, thanks for making it easy. I am not so interested either. I wouldn't wanna date someone who replies a day after. That is just not normal. You people are so damn racist toward foreigners. If someone is foreign you just think he is got to be no good. But that is your problem not mine.

> Me: I responded to you today after you sent me a text today. Plus, I've explained previously, I'm busy with the play and work. Plus my response time is NORMAL. What isn't normal is someone being so demanding of someone else when they don't even really know the person. We obviously have different ideas of normal and expectations. Many of my closest friends are not native to the U.S. So that assumption you placed on me being racist is completely false. I was being respectful by not wasting your time and money if I am not interested.

> (928) BAD-DATE: If you are gonna judge a person based on a short meeting like we did than prejudice must have played a role.

> Me: There was no judging and no prejudice. Just no chemistry. It is not negative or personal. It just is. You seem like a nice guy and I wish you luck. This conversation has run its course and I don't think there is a need for any further contact.

> (928) BAD-DATE: I was also open for short term dating. I haven't dated many white American girls and you probably haven't dated foreigners. So it could have been good experience for both of us.

30 minutes later...

> 10:34 p.m.

> (928) BAD-DATE: Ohhh please like I am dying to keep contacting you. And by the way for your info if I don't keep texting for a response and don't care that when you are gonna reply then that is not called demanding.

HUH??

Random Creep   Me

I met him at the corner bar. I was with a neighbor. He was there with a friend. The four of us had a snowball fight. In the middle of the snowball fight, our mutual friends started making out. Later that night, this is what I get:

10:29 p.m.

> (917) BAD-DATE - Your dear friend Shane from 51st St

I didn't respond

11:12 p.m.

> (917) BAD-DATE - And if I told u we were ok with open marriage. Would u invite me up for a nightcap.

I never responded. I still haven't learned to be more careful about handing out my business cards!

Coming Full Circle... Maybe!

I never thought I would be in my forties and still be looking for that person to share my life with. I was tired of the games and nonsense. I just wanted someone normal enough who wanted me.

Wrong Wayne   Me

Wayne was very honest from the beginning. He said he didn't want a relationship, only a companion. He didn't want to get married because he'd been there, done that, and had three kids. He wasn't even my type. He was ten years older and I wasn't physically attracted to him. So, imagine my surprise when we actually hit it off!

In the beginning, there were non-stop emails for weeks. I honestly liked the attention. It took him a month or so of wooing and charming me before I would even go out with him. The date was great! The emails continued. Then we went on more dinner and lunch dates. They were great! The conversations were great! The sex was great! He would carry my bag, open doors, stand up when I arrived at the table. I had not been with anyone where we were so immensely compatible. It was just amazing every time.

While the chase was on, scheduling seemed easier than after he caught me. His flexibility and availability diminished with excuses of his job, traveling frequently, and being a helicopter parent for his kids.

I needed to end "this" because the enjoyment of the physical relationship was not frequent enough to override the frustration regarding the lack of dates and attention. I knew the relationship was open and I could date other men. I thought I had evolved enough to have this type of non-relationship until the right one came along. I guess I was wrong.

But I chose to hold onto this relationship somewhat selfishly for the next couple of months because my birthday was coming up. I was hoping for a present after the months of the tumultuous ups and downs of this relationship. I got NADA. I was hurt. Why? The writing was clearly on the wall. He was clear what the relationship was and wasn't from the beginning. It was obvious he really didn't care. I had in the last months started casually seeing someone. I decided after nothing special for my birthday, I was done and ended it. I told him I had met someone else and wanted to make it exclusive. Ironically, Wayne was jealous tried to woo me back with expensive dinners and wine. The chase was back on, but too little too late and he still didn't want to be exclusive.

Brother Benjamin   **Him**
The One Who Got Away #1-1/2
Love of my Life #4

Literally, as I was editing the first Brother Benjamin entry in this book, I looked down at my phone and saw a notification on LinkedIn from Ben congratulating me on a work anniversary. I hadn't heard from him in about three years, ever since he left Facebook. I messaged him back to tell him what a coincidence this was since I was just talking with a friend about him. I certainly couldn't tell him about the book! So, after a little back and forth, I found out that he was divorced, lived in Charlotte, North Carolina, and was a National Sales Manager.

Turned out he was in Philadelphia on business and invited me down for the day. I was supposed to visit my mother, but in another coincidence, those plans fell through. So, I hopped on the next train and met him. He hadn't changed much except he had a little less hair and had put on a few pounds.

We really hit it off. It was like we had just seen each other yesterday. We had a great time exploring the city together and he had thoughtfully booked a hotel room with two beds in case I wanted to spend the night. I did, and yes, we did make out.

The next time he came back to Philadelphia, he took a side trip to New York afterwards. Again, we had a really great time together.

We continued talking and emailing each other. Since Ben could work from any city for his job, he traveled to New York at least once a month. Twice he stayed for a week. Since I was either at work or in class during that time, he made me dinner every night and did all the food shopping. He started running to get into better shape. We explored Manhattan together and met up with a few friends. They thought he was terrific! Now I understood what people meant when they said it should be easy. I couldn't believe how quickly things fell into place.

Ben wanted to check out where he grew up, so he came home with me for my birthday weekend. He met some of my friends and family and they adored him. He saw all the Super Girl stuff I owned and bought me a t-shirt, socks, and a keychain to add to my collection. It was thoughtful!

We drove around the old neighborhood reminiscing about high school and people we knew. He remembered me visiting his sister and all the hickeys he gave me! He said, "Remember making out in the backseat of the red Toyota in the school parking lot?" I guffawed "That was you? I had remembered making out with someone in a red car but couldn't remember who it was." We laughed a lot. At this point I didn't need Wayne anymore, and I broke up with him. (See previous entry.)

My relationship with Ben blossomed despite it being a long-distance one. I would get a "good morning" and a "goodnight" text or phone call daily. He would send me small gifts that reminded him of me and links to YouTube videos of songs that would make him think of me.

I visited him in Charlotte in the Fall. Ben lived in a nice suburban cookie-cutter area that was so NOT me! I am a city girl. He understood that and said that he could live any place where there is an airport but wanted to keep the house for another year since his son was moving back once he graduated college.

I met a few of his friends and we all got along great. They were teasing Ben about needing to carry a fanny pack because he was whipped. On my next visit, I brought them all matching camouflage fanny packs.

Over the winter months, our relationship continued to grow. We talked openly to each other. Even during arguments, we were always able to work things out. He told me that as a teen, he saw an old man walking his dog and he thought, "That will be me someday." But he really wanted to grow old with his best friend. This seemed to be the direction we were heading.

He was so sweet and romantic. It was clear that finishing school was a priority for me and he was supportive of that decision. He said it often. He would even help me with assignments. Ben knew I had two years of graduate school and a one-year internship. His motto was "Ain't' in no rush for nuthin'!" Ben took me by surprise by sending me an email with internships in the Charlotte area that he had researched unbeknownst to me.

We talked about living together. Then we talked about marriage. He didn't want any more kids and I didn't want any at this age. He told me I was like no one he ever met before. He appreciated that. He told me he loved me and that I was the strong, independent women he wanted and needed. I was truly in love. It finally all came together. I had my new career, a self-made man who enjoyed his career and was unbelievably supportive, kind, and loving. He fell in love with me. I felt I could exhale. I DID. This was a successful long-distance relationship that was working. He did not smoke pot. We had many "Sex in the City" moments from him grabbing me in the apartment to dance to random songs to me showing PDA.

In February, I flew out to San Diego to meet him at a convention. I met some of his co-workers who were very nice, but I didn't have anything in common with the wives. They were busy being stay-at-home moms and getting their nails, spray tans, and eyelashes done. I am just not that kind of woman. Kids are out of the picture for me and I would rather be hiking than getting a manicure.

In March, he decided to stop jogging. He proclaimed he was an "all or nothing" guy, and since he couldn't commit 100%, he wouldn't exercise at all. I loved him as he was, but I had concerns about his health. At least he did start to eat better and began to lose weight.

During my Spring break, we went to my mom's cottage for a week. My nieces adored him. He taught them to fish and let them sit in the front seat of the pickup while we sat in the back seat at the drive-in.

On our way back to New York, he told me that he liked where he was living and had no plans to ever sell his house. So, now his tune changed from "I can live anywhere" to "I'm not leaving my house." It was like Lance telling me he wanted to quit smoking pot and put me as his focus, but then realized that either he couldn't do it or didn't want to do it.

Ben's work started picking up and it became more difficult for him to plan time to see me. The communication also dwindled. I told him I missed the songs he used to send. He said he doesn't listen to music much anymore. I told him that our relationship was not like it was when we first were dating. His response was, "Relationships evolve." Okay, I really didn't want to address all that since I was in the middle of finals.

I went to Charlotte to see him just after school ended. We were flying in at the same time, so we met at the airport. He had been sick for the past week so when we met, he was a bit lackluster, showing no excitement to see me. I felt bad for him because I knew he hadn't been feeling well. When we got to his house, his son was there with his dog. Ben perked up immediately and was more excited to see the dog than he was to see me. I told him that hurt my feelings. He said I was overreacting and I would be excited if it were my dog. Not the best way to start the weekend!

When it came to having sex that evening, he said he really wasn't interested in sex anymore. He had mentioned this before, but good grief! It's only once a month! So here I am, a woman in my forties who is peaking sexually, who waited a month, only to be rejected. I let it go and the rest of the weekend was fine.

Over the next week, I tried to coordinate our next meetup. I was on break from school so it was easy for me to travel there if he couldn't swing New York with his work schedule. We talked on the phone on Friday. As I was telling him about my rotten day and how frustrated I was, he fell asleep on me! I was pissed but sent him a nicely written text saying I was upset about it. He finally called me the next evening and didn't say a word about falling asleep on me, or the text. I was livid!

I stewed on it then called him the next morning and got right to it. He said he didn't understand why we couldn't "just be natural and have it all work out?" He and his buddy can "just be and it's fine." I said ,"You should try fucking your buddy and see how that changes things!". He came back saying "I don't believe in working on relationships. They should just happen." This explains why he is twice divorced.

We continued to talk and we seemed to work things out. We agreed that when he is in bed, I would not talk about anything important. He had to go because his "just be buddy" was waiting for him while we were on the phone. I told him he should have said something and we could have worked it out later. He said he would call later to finish it up.

Well, later came and went and no call. The next day there was no morning call nor text. I did receive a text from him about 8pm asking me if I was available. I wasn't at that time. I called him when I got home and he said, "I don't think I am the right person for you. I cannot meet your expectations and you should find someone who can." I asked, "Is this a discussion or a decision?" "It's a discussion" he said. I replied, "There are very few people who can meet my expectations and if I am putting too much on you, tell me what it is and I can tell you whether it's a deal breaker for me." He was silent. I asked, "What are the expectations that are too high for you to meet?" He finally replied, "You are trying too hard to set up a schedule for us to see each other." In reality, I was only asking for a once a month visit and a text/brief call for good morning and good night. I said, "We are still learning about each other. Our schedules are in such flux with me finishing Grad school and you getting into the groove of your new position. Things will change again in a year when I start an internship." All I could think is he is the one who said "Ain't in no rush for nuthin," right?

We didn't break up that night, but this really knocked the wind out of my sails. I was devastated. I felt he really needed some space and tried my best to give it to him. I didn't text him as much and we didn't talk every day. For a couple of weeks, things seemed to be working out okay. We would talk and laugh. Things seemed to be getting back to normal. Wind started filling up the sails.

When I brought up the subject of us seeing each other, he said he didn't know his work schedule and wouldn't charge his company for an open-ended ticket just so he could come to New York. OUCH! Since I was still on break, I asked about me coming to Charlotte. He said that didn't even cross his mind as an option. Really? There went the sails again. I remembered my friends who gave their husbands the space while dating. I tried this tactic again with Ben just as I tried with Perfect Pete.

After this conversation, he didn't call, email or text me the whole next day. I sent him a good night text and a "good morning sun" emoji. Later that day, he called me and said, "This isn't a good call..."

Yep, he broke up with me. He said we were moving in different directions and he needed to focus on his job. He repeated that he couldn't meet my expectations and I needed to find someone who could. I reminded him that he was giving up his dream of growing old with his best friend. He said he knew that but refused to tell me what triggered the change in him. He said he didn't know how to say it any differently. So, I said "OK it's done. I wish you the best" and hung up. I sent him a text later thanking him for a wonderful 10 ½ months and for his support and love. I never heard back from him.

I spent the following day crying in bed watching "Schitt's Creek." I told myself "Only one full day of this!" Okay, I did spend several half-days and quarter-days crying, but not a full day! My dream was shattered and my heart was in pieces. It is amazing how my network of friends came together to help a sister through this. Even my nieces pitched in! They really liked Ben and were so mad that he broke my heart. The youngest one said, "I hope he looks at everything you gave him and the bookmark I made for him and sees what a jerk he is." They touched my heart something fierce.

I thought I was done dating and had my best friend to grow old with. I had been dating for 35 years looking for that companion who loved me as much as I loved him. For the second time of my life, I thought I was there. He morphed into the person who turned his back on the dream that we shared. But I have come to realize that he didn't give up anything. Early in our relationship, he said "I dream of growing old with my best friend but I can't help seeing myself as a single old man walking his dog," I see now that they are one in the same. I just didn't think that when he said best friend, he meant the dog. I thought he meant me.

Lil' Muddy Paws

I met Muddy Paws through a friend and he's my current flame. He really didn't fit my type but he was a youngin', and I melted when I saw those doe eyes! On our first date, he was so happy to meet me and showered me with hugs and kisses (no tongue, thank God!). When we would walk down the street together, strangers would comment how cute he is! And I was okay with it because he is sooo cute! Things progressed quickly and he moved in with me. He is full of kisses and never gets mad at me. He can be a bit stubborn but we never go to bed mad. When we settle in for the night, he always gives me a kiss and a cuddle. I can always count on him being by my side and protecting me. He will keep me happy and warm until we get to that final chapter.

So, what will the sequel be?

Hopefully only one more chapter.

www.ingramcontent.com/pod-product-compliance
Lightning Source LLC
Chambersburg PA
CBHW071218070526
44584CB00019B/3070